LITIGATION STYLES:
FAMILY ACTIONS
AND ADOPTION

Alison Stirling, MA (Hons), LLB
Advocate

A handy and practical aid for those who have responsibility for drafting pleadings in the Scottish Courts, this volume brings together a collection of styles for litigation in the Sheriff Court and Court of Session. Included are styles originally published in *Greens Litigation Styles*, edited by Lord Carloway, and additional valuable new styles.

W. GREEN

THOMSON REUTERS

Published in 2010
by W. Green & Son Limited
21 Alva Street
Edinburgh EH2 4PS

Typeset by YHT Ltd, Hillingdon
Printed and bound in Great Britain by CPI Anthony Rowe,
Chippenham and Eastbourne

No natural forests were destroyed to make this product;
only farmed timber was used and replanted.

A CIP catalogue record of this book is available from the British
Library.

ISBN 978-0-414-01847-1

LITIGATION STYLES:
FAMILY ACTIONS
AND ADOPTION

CONTENTS

Page

F01: DECLARATORS

F02: DIVORCE, DISSOLUTION OF CIVIL PARTNERSHIPS AND SEPARATION

Divorce

Contents vii

F04: ADOPTION

DECLARATORS

IN THE COURT OF SESSION

SUMMONS

in the cause

[*name, designation and address*], Pursuer

against

[*names, designations and addresses*], Defenders

CONCLUSION

For declarator that the pursuer and the late [*name of deceased*] were lawfully married to one another by cohabitation at [*address or addresses in Scotland*] from [*date when parties were free to marry and were in Scotland*] until the death of [*name of deceased*] on [*date*] and the habit and repute arising therefrom.

CONDESCENDENCE

I. The pursuer resides at [*address*]. The first defender[1] resides at [*address*]. He is the son of the deceased [*name*] by his marriage to [*name*]. The second defender resides at [*address*]. He is the son of the late [*name*] and the pursuer. The pursuer has been habitually resident in Scotland throughout the period of one year ending with the date of the commencement of this action.[2] To the knowledge of the pursuer no proceedings are continuing in Scotland or elsewhere in respect of the marriage to which this action relates or are capable of affecting its validity or subsistence.[3]

II. The pursuer met [*the deceased*] around [*date*]. At that time [*the deceased*] was married, but lived apart from [*name*]. The pursuer and [*the deceased*] developed a close

F01–01   relationship and began living together in or about [*date*] at
[*address*]. The marriage of [*the deceased*] to [*name*] was
dissolved on [*date*].

   III. Following the dissolution of the marriage of [*the deceased*]
the pursuer and [*the deceased*] lived together as husband
and wife at [*address or addresses*] until the death of [*the
deceased*] on [*date*].[4] Their son, [*name*], the second defender,
was born on [*date*]. The pursuer was known as
"Mrs [*name*]". The pursuer's name appeared as "[*name*]"
on the electoral register and on the register of a general
medical practitioner. Neighbours and friends regarded the
pursuer and [*the deceased*] as husband and wife. On social
occasions [*the deceased*] introduced the pursuer as his wife.

   IV. In the circumstances the pursuer desires to have it
declared that she was lawfully married to the late [*the
deceased*].

PLEA-IN-LAW

The pursuer and the said [*name*] having lived together as husband and wife and having been regarded as such, the pursuer is
entitled to decree of declarator as concluded for.

IN RESPECT WHEREOF

---

[1] The defender to an action of declarator of marriage may be the other party,
if still alive. The style of conclusion in such a case is that found at R.C. Form
13.2B(10). In some circumstances the Lord Advocate may be called as defender
as representing the public interest.

[2] Domicile and Matrimonial Proceedings Act 1973, s.7(3).

[3] R.C. 49.2.

[4] There are various cases on the length and quality of cohabitation necessary
to entitle a pursuer to the remedy sought. The assessment of the particular
situation is basically a matter for the court (see Clive, *Husband and Wife* (4th
ed.), pp.52–55).

Marriage—Nullity—Defender's impotency[1]   F01–02

IN THE COURT OF SESSION

SUMMONS

in the cause

[*name and address*] (also known as "Mrs [*name*]
or [*name*]"), pursuer

against

[*name and address*], defender

CONCLUSIONS

FIRST.   For declarator that a pretended marriage between
the pursuer and defender at [*place*] on [*date*] is null
by reason of the defender's impotency.

SECOND. For the expenses of the action in the event of
opposition.

CONDESCENDENCE

I. The pursuer resides at [*address*]. The defender resides at
[*address*]. The pursuer has been habitually resident in
Scotland throughout the period of one year ending with
the date of the commencement of this action.[2] This court
accordingly has jurisdiction. There are no proceedings
continuing in Scotland or elsewhere in respect of the
pretended marriage to which this action relates or which
are capable of affecting its validity or subsistence.[3]

II. The pursuer and the defender went through a pretended
form of marriage at [*place*] on [*date*]. An extract certificate
of [*the registration relative to the ceremony*] is produced
herewith.

III. At the time of said ceremony, the pursuer was willing and
anxious that the marriage should be consummated. She

wished to start a family with the defender and to enjoy full marital relations with him.

IV. Shortly after the ceremony, the pursuer and the defender left on honeymoon to [*place*]. On the first night of the honeymoon, the pursuer made it clear to the defender that she wanted sexual intercourse to take place between them. The defender made an excuse that he was tired and would not permit the pursuer to make sexual advances to him. Over the subsequent few days, the pursuer attempted to interest the defender in having sexual relations with her but the defender always put her off with an excuse. The period of honeymoon ended without the marriage being consummated. The pursuer and the defender then returned to the marital home which at that time was at [*address*].

V. The pursuer was upset and depressed by the above situation. She attempted to discuss matters with the defender and finally persuaded him that he should see their doctor about his apparent unwillingness or inability to consummate the marriage. The parties' general practitioner, Dr [*name*], and Dr [*name*], a consultant psychiatrist, were consulted. There is no physical reason why the defender should be incapable of consummating the marriage, but the defender has an invincible repugnancy to sexual relations, at least with the pursuer.

VI. Following on receipt of reports from Dr [*name*] and Dr [*name*] and on the continued refusal by or inability of the defender to have sexual relations with her, the pursuer considered the pretended marriage to be at an end. She left the defender on or about [*date*] and has not cohabited with him since.

VII. At the date of the marriage ceremony the defender was incapable of sexual intercourse with the pursuer. He is still is incapable of having sexual intercourse with the pursuer. He knew that the pursuer was willing and anxious that they should have carnal connection. In these circumstances the pursuer seeks decree of declarator as concluded for.

PLEA-IN-LAW

The defender being, at the time of the marriage, permanently and incurably incapable of consummating the marriage, decree of nullity should be granted as concluded for.

IN RESPECT WHEREOF

---

[1] An action on the ground of impotency can also be brought at the instance of an *incapax* pursuer.

[2] See the Domicile and Matrimonial Proceedings Act 1973 s.7(3A) for alternative grounds of jurisdiction.

[3] See RCS 49.2 for where there are such proceedings.

F01–03   **Marriage—Nullity—Lack of consent**

IN THE COURT OF SESSION

SUMMONS

in the cause

[*name, designation and address*], Pursuer

against

[*name, designation and address*], Defender

CONCLUSION

For declarator that a pretended marriage between the pursuer and defender at [*place*] on [*date*] is null by reason of lack of consent of the pursuer, the pretended marriage having been entered into under duress.

CONDESCENDENCE

I. The pursuer resides at [*address*]. The defender resides at [*address*]. The pursuer has been habitually resident in Scotland throughout the period of one year ending with the date of commencement of this action.[1] There are no proceedings continuing in Scotland or elsewhere in respect of the pretended marriage to which this action relates or are capable of affecting its validity or subsistence.[2]

II. On [*date*] the pursuer went through a pretended form of marriage with the defender at [*place*]. An extract certificate of the marriage is produced. Both parties were brought up in the Muslim religion. At the time of the marriage the pursuer was [*age*] years old. The marriage was arranged by the parties' parents. The pursuer did not freely consent to the marriage. Her family had applied pressure on her for some time to marry the defender. Initially she had resisted the pressure. However her parents proceeded to arrange a marriage ceremony despite the pursuer's unwillingness. Shortly before the date of the ceremony the pursuer's parents informed her that they would exclude her from the

family home if she persisted in her refusal to marry the **F01–03**
defender. She had no alternative accommodation. She had
no means with which to support herself independently of
her family. She was fearful of disobeying her parents.
During the previous year, one of her female cousins had
refused to enter into an arranged marriage. She had been
ostracised by her extended family and by the local Muslim
community.

III. On the day of the arranged marriage ceremony the pursuer was anxious and upset. She attempted to leave the
family home in the morning but her father physically
prevented her from doing so. She was taken by her parents to the registry office at [*place*] where the marriage
ceremony took place.

IV. Following the ceremony the pursuer and the defender
went to live at the home of the pursuer's parents. They
purchased a flatted dwelling-house in joint names on
[*date*]. The pursuer has lived there since then. On or about
[*date*] the defender went to England to work for relatives.
He has resided in Birmingham since then. The parties
have not cohabited or had marital relations since [*date*].

V. The pursuer never consented to the marriage and now
seeks to have it annulled on the grounds that she entered
into it under duress.

PLEA-IN-LAW

The pretended marriage having been entered into whilst the
pursuer was under duress and without her consent declarator
should be pronounced as concluded for.

IN RESPECT WHEREOF

---

[1] Domicile and Matrimonial Proceedings Act 1973, s. 7(3).
[2] R.C. 49.2.

IN THE COURT OF SESSION

SUMMONS

in the cause

[*name, designation and address*], Pursuer

against

[*name, designation and address*], Defender

CONCLUSION

For declarator that a pretended marriage between the pursuer and the defender at [*place*] on [*date*] is null on the ground that at the time of the pretended marriage the defender was married and still is married to [*name*], residing at [*address*].

CONDESCENDENCE

I. The pursuer resides at [*address*]. The defender resides at [*address*]. The pursuer has been habitually resident in Scotland throughout the period of one year ending with the date of the commencement of this action.[1] There are no proceedings continuing in Scotland or elsewhere in respect of the pretended marriage to which this action relates or are capable of affecting its validity or subsistence.[2]

II. On [*date*] the pursuer went through a pretended form of marriage with the defender at [*place*]. The pursuer thought at the time she was contracting a regular marriage with the defender. An extract certificate of the marriage is produced. After the ceremony the pursuer and the defender took up residence together at [*address*] where they lived as husband and wife until [*date*] when, in consequence of the matters hereinafter condescended upon, the pursuer left the defender. She has not seen him since then.

III. Three years after the date of the ceremony, the pursuer **F01–04**
received information to the effect that the defender had
been married before and that his wife was still alive. On
investigating the matter she ascertained (as was in fact the
case) that on [*date*] at [*place*] the defender married [*name*],
presently residing at [*address*]. This marriage has never
been dissolved.

IV. In the circumstances the pursuer's pretended marriage
with the defender was a nullity and she seeks to have it so
declared.

PLEA-IN-LAW

The pretended marriage being null and void by reason of the
previous and still subsisting marriage of the defender,
declarator of nullity should be pronounced as concluded for.

IN RESPECT WHEREOF

---

[1] Domicile and Matrimonial Proceedings Act 1973, s. 7(3).
[2] R.C. 49.2.

IN THE COURT OF SESSION

SUMMONS

in the cause

[*name and address*]
(also known as "Mrs [*name*] or [*name*]"), Pursuer

against

[*name and address*], Defender

CONCLUSIONS

FIRST.For declarator that a pretended marriage between the pursuer and defender at [*place*] on [*date*] is null by reason of the defender being married to someone else.

SECOND.   For the expenses of the action.

CONDESCENDENCE

I. The pursuer resides at [*address*]. The defender resides at [*address*]. The pursuer has been habitually resident in Scotland throughout the period of one year ending with the date of the commencement of this action. There are no proceedings continuing in Scotland or elsewhere in respect of the pretended marriage to which this action relates or are capable of affecting its validity or sub-sistence.

II. The pursuer and the defender went through a pretended form of marriage at [*place*] on [*date*]. An extract of the relative certificate of registration is produced.

III. After the ceremony, the pursuer and the defender lived together at the defender's present address. On or about [*date*], the defender confessed to the pursuer that, at the time of said ceremony, he was already married to [*name*], he having gone through a valid ceremony of marriage

with [*name*] at [*place*] on [*date*]. The defender's confession **F01–05**
was true. The pursuer was distressed by this disclosure
and decided that she could no longer reside with the
defender. She therefore left him on or about [*date*]. An
extract certificate of the registration of the defender's prior
subsisting marriage is produced. The matter has now been
reported by the pursuer to the appropriate authorities for
them to consider whether criminal action against the
defender is justified.

IV. The pursuer seeks to have the pretended marriage
declared a nullity.

PLEA-IN-LAW

The pretended marriage being null and void by reason of the
previous and still subsisting marriage of the defender declarator
of nullity should be pronounced as concluded for.

IN RESPECT WHEREOF

F01–06   **Civil partnership—Nullity—Lack of consent—Error**

IN THE COURT OF SESSION

SUMMONS

in the cause

[*name and address*], Pursuer

against

[*name and address*], Defender

CONCLUSION

For declarator that a pretended civil partnership between the pursuer and defender registered at [*place*] on [*date*] is null by reason of lack of consent of the pursuer, the pretended civil partnership having been entered into by reason only of error.

CONDESCENDENCE

I. The pursuer resides at [*address*]. The defender resides at [*address*]. The pursuer is habitually resident in Scotland and has resided in Scotland for at least one year immediately preceding the date on which this action was commenced.[1] There are no proceedings continuing in Scotland or elsewhere in respect of the pretended civil partnership to which this action relates or which are capable of affecting its validity or subsistence.[2]

II. On [*date*] the pursuer went through a pretended form of civil partnership with the defender at [*place*]. An extract of the relevant entry in the civil partnership register is produced herewith.

III. The parties met each other through a social networking site on the internet. The social networking site encouraged diverse persons from all over Europe to communicate on line with each other. The pursuer communicated with a number of such persons through the internet. She had not met the defender in person prior to the ceremony to register the civil partnership. The pursuer thought that she **F01–06** was entering into a civil partnership with [*name and address*] whom she had also met on line. She had agreed to register a civil partnership with [*name*]. She was not aware that the defender was not [*name*] until after she had purported to register the civil partnership with her.

IV. Following the ceremony the pursuer realised that the defender was not the woman with whom she had agreed to register a civil partnership. The pursuer would not have registered a civil partnership with the defender had she known the defender was not [*name*]. The parties have not cohabited since [*date*].

V. The pursuer never consented to the civil partnership with the defender and now seeks to have it annulled on the grounds that she entered into it in error.

PLEA-IN-LAW

The pretended civil partnership having been entered into by the pursuer by reason only of error and without her consent, decree of declarator should be pronounced as concluded for.

IN RESPECT WHEREOF

---

[1] See the Civil Partnership Act 2004 s.225(3) and the Civil Partnership (Jurisdiction and Recognition of Judgments) (Scotland) Regulations 2005 for alternative grounds of jurisdiction.

[2] See RCS 49.2 for where there are such proceedings.

F01–07 Civil partnership—Nullity—Prior subsisting civil partnership

IN THE COURT OF SESSION

SUMMONS

in the cause

[*name and address*], pursuer

against

[*name and address*], defender

CONCLUSION

For declarator that a pretended civil partnership between the pursuer and defender registered at [*place*] on [*date*] is null on the ground that at the time of the pretended civil partnership the defender was and still is the civil partner of [*name*], residing at [*address*].

CONDESCENDENCE

I. The pursuer resides at [*address*]. The defender resides at [*address*]. The pursuer is habitually resident in Scotland and has resided in Scotland for at least one year immediately preceding the date on which this action was commenced.[1] There are no proceedings continuing in Scotland or elsewhere in respect of the pretended civil partnership to which this action relates or which are capable of affecting its validity or subsistence.[2]

II. On [*date*] the pursuer went through a pretended form of civil partnership with the defender at [*place*]. An extract of the relevant entry in the civil partnership register is produced herewith.

III. The pursuer thought at the time that he was contracting a valid civil partnership with the defender. After the ceremony the pursuer and the defender took up residence together at [*address*] where they lived as civil partners until [*date*] when, in consequence of the matters hereinafter

condescended upon, the pursuer left the defender. He has **F01–07**
not seen him since then.

IV. Three years after the date of the ceremony the pursuer
received information to the effect that the defender had
previously registered a civil partnership with another man
and that his civil partner was still alive. On investigating
the matter the pursuer ascertained (as was in fact the case)
that on [*date*] at [*place*] the defender registered a civil
partnership with [*name*], presently residing at [*address*].
This civil partnership has never been dissolved.

V. In the circumstances the pursuer's pretended civil partnership with the defender was a nullity and he seeks to
have it so declared.

PLEA-IN-LAW

The pretended civil partnership being null and void by reason
of the previous and still subsisting civil partnership of the
defender, decree of declarator should be pronounced as concluded for.

IN RESPECT WHEREOF

---

[1] See the Civil Partnership Act 2004 s.225(3) and the Civil Partnership
(Jurisdiction and Recognition of Judgments) (Scotland) Regulations 2005 for
alternative grounds of jurisdiction.
[2] See RCS 49.2 where there are such proceedings.

IN THE COURT OF SESSION

SUMMONS

in the cause

[*name and address*], pursuer

against

[*names and addresses*][1], defenders

CONCLUSION

To find and declare that [*name and address*] is not the parent of [*name and date of birth*], residing at [*address*].

CONDESCENDENCE

I. The pursuer resides at [*address*]. The first and second defenders reside at [*address*]. [*The third defender is the Child Maintenance and Enforcement Commission, a body corporate established under the Child Maintenance and Other Payments Act 2008. The third defender has a place of business at (address).*] The pursuer is domiciled in Scotland. He has been habitually resident in Scotland for more than one year immediately before the raising of this action[2]. This court accordingly has jurisdiction.

II. The pursuer and the first defender were married at [*place*] on [*date*]. On [*date*] their child, [*name*], was born. The marriage became unhappy. Around [*date*] the pursuer went to work in Germany. He returned to Scotland on [*date*]. He stayed with the first defender for around two weeks. They had marital relations with each other. Thereafter they separated, since when they have neither lived together nor had marital relations. On [*date*] the first defender gave birth to a child, [*name*], the second defender. The first defender registered the birth of the second defender in the Register of Births, Marriages and Deaths. Extract registered certificate is produced. The pursuer

initially had no knowledge of the birth of the second **F01–08**
defender. As husband of the first defender, the pursuer is
presumed to be the father of the second defender.

III. On [*date*] the first defender applied for a maintenance
calculation under s.4 of the Child Support Act 1991.
A maintenance calculation was made under s.11 of that
Act and on [*date*] the pursuer was ordered to pay the sum
of £[*amount in figures*] per week in respect of the two
children [name] and the second defender.

IV. The pursuer is not the parent of the second defender. The
first defender has admitted that the pursuer is not the
father of the second defender. The pursuer has requested
that the first and second defenders provide samples of
blood or other body fluid or body tissue to enable DNA
testing to be carried out, but the first defender has refused
to co-operate by providing such samples. In the circumstances the pursuer seeks declarator that he is not the
parent of the second defender.

PLEA-IN-LAW

The pursuer, not being the parent of the second defender, is
entitled to declarator as concluded for.

IN RESPECT WHEREOF

---

[1] The child whose parentage is under review should be called as a defender:
Jamieson v Jamieson, 1969 S.L.T. (Notes) 11. Where there is a maintenance calculation in terms of the Child Support Act 1991, the Child Maintenance and
Enforcement Commission should be called as a defender: s.28 of the 1991 Act
as amended by the Child Maintenance and Other Payments Act 2008 s.3(4),
Sch.3, Sch.8. See also RCS 49.6(4)(b) and 49.82.
[2] Law Reform (Parent and Child) (Scotland) Act 1986 s.7.

IN THE COURT OF SESSION

DEFENCES

for the First Defender

in the cause

[*name and address*], Pursuer

against

[*name and address*], First Defender

and

[*name and address*], Second Defender

and

The Child Maintenance and Enforcement Commission,
[*address*], Third Defender

ANSWERS TO CONDESCENDENCE FOR FIRST DEFENDER

I. Admitted.

II. Admitted that the pursuer and first defender were married at [*place*] on [*date*] and that on [*date*] their child, [*name*], was born. Admitted that the marriage became unhappy. Admitted that the pursuer went to work in Germany for a time. Admitted that the first defender gave birth to the second defender on [*date*] and that the birth of the second defender was registered by the first defender. Reference is made to the extract registered certificate of birth produced. *Quoad ultra* denied except in so far as coinciding herewith. Explained and averred that, on his return from Germany on or about [*date*], the pursuer resumed cohabitation with the first defender. Thereafter, they lived together as man and wife for a period of approximately six months until they separated finally in or about [*date*]. The

pursuer is the father of the second defender. The second **F01–09**
defender was conceived during the period when the
parties were residing together as man and wife, although
the second defender was born after the date of final
separation. The first defender wrote to the pursuer to
advise him of the birth of the second defender although
the pursuer has since denied that he is the father and
refuses to support the second defender.

III. Admitted that the first defender applied for a maintenance
calculation under the Child Support Act 1991. Believed to
be true that the pursuer has since been required to make
payments in support of the second defender. *Quoad ultra*
not known and not admitted.

IV. Admitted that the pursuer denies paternity of the second
defender. Admitted that the pursuer has requested that
the first defender and the second defender provide samples of blood to enable DNA testing to be carried out.
Admitted that the first pursuer is unwilling to provide
such samples and to give permission for similar samples
to be taken from the second defender. *Quoad ultra* denied
except in so far as coinciding herewith. Explained and
averred that tests are unnecessary. The pursuer has
admitted paternity of the second defender. He denied
paternity only when required under the Child Support
Act 1991 to pay maintenance in respect of the second
defender.

PLEA-IN-LAW FOR FIRST DEFENDER

The pursuer being the parent of the second defender, decree of
declarator should be refused.

IN RESPECT WHEREOF

　　　　　　Non-parentage—Sheriff court

SHERIFFDOM OF [*sheriffdom*]
AT [*place*]

INITIAL WRIT

In the cause

[*name and address*], pursuer

Against

[*names and addresses*],[1] defenders

The Pursuer craves the court to find and declare that [*name and address*] is not the parent of [*name and date of birth*], residing at [*address*].

CONDESCENDENCE

I. The pursuer resides at [*address*]. The first and second defenders reside at [*address*]. [The third defender is the Child Maintenance and Enforcement Commission, a body corporate established under the Child Maintenance and Other Payments Act 2008. The third defender has a place of business at [*address*].] The pursuer is domiciled in Scotland. He has been habitually resident in Scotland for more than one year immediately before the raising of this action. The pursuer is habitually resident in this sheriffdom at the date of the commencement of this action.[2] This court accordingly has jurisdiction.

II. The pursuer and the first defender were married at [*place*] on [*date*]. On [*date*] their child [*name*] was born. The marriage became unhappy. Around [*date*] the pursuer went to work in Germany. He returned to Scotland on [*date*]. He stayed with the first defender for around two weeks. They had marital relations. Thereafter they separated, since when they have neither lived together nor had marital relations. On [*date*] the first defender gave birth to a child, [*name*], the second defender. The first defender registered the birth of the second defender in the Register of Births, Marriages and Deaths. Extract registered certificate is produced. The pursuer initially had no knowledge of the **F01–10** birth of the second defender. As husband of the first defender, the pursuer is presumed to be the father of the second defender.

III. On [*date*] the first defender applied for a maintenance calculation under section 4 of the Child Support Act 1991. A maintenance calculation was made under section 11 of that Act and on [*date*] the pursuer was ordered to pay the sum of £[*amount in figures*] per week in respect of the two children [*name*] and the second defender.

IV. The pursuer is not the parent of the second defender. The first defender has admitted that the pursuer is not the father of the second defender. The pursuer has requested that the first and second defenders provide samples of blood or other body fluid or body tissue to enable DNA testing to be carried out, but the first defender has refused to co-operate by providing such samples. In the circumstances the pursuer seeks declarator that he is not the parent of the second defender.

PLEA-IN-LAW

The pursuer, not being the parent of the second defender, is entitled to declarator as craved.

IN RESPECT WHEREOF

---

[1] The child whose parentage is under review should be called as a defender: *Jamieson v Jamieson*, 1969 S.L.T. (Notes) 11. Where there is a maintenance calculation in terms of the Child Support Act 1991 the Child Maintenance and Enforcement Commission should be called as a defender: s.28 of the 1991 Act as amended by the Child Maintenance and Other Payments Act 2008 s.13(4), Sch.3, Sch.8. See also OCR 33.6(4)(b) and 33.89.

[2] Law Reform (Parent and Child) (Scotland) Act 1986, s.7.

DIVORCE, DISSOLUTION OF CIVIL PARTNERSHIP AND SEPARATION

Warrant to intimate to [*name and address*] as a child of the marriage (or to [*name and address*] as a child who has been accepted by both partners of a civil partnership as a child of the family) and to [*name and address*] the [*state relationship to defender*], as one of the next-of-kin of the defender.

Warrant to intimate to [*name and address*] as a person with whom the defender is alleged to have committed adultery.

To [grant warrant to] intimate to [*name and address*] as a child of the marriage (or to [*name and address*] as a child who has been accepted by both partners of a civil partnership as a child of the family), [*name and address*] the [*relationship to the defender*] as one of the next-of-kin of the defender, [*name and address*], curator bonis to the defender and [*name and address*] guardian (or continuing (or welfare) attorney) to the defender."

To [grant warrant to] intimate to [*name and address*] as an additional spouse of the pursuer (or the defender).

Warrant to intimate to [*name and address*], as a child who may be affected by the action.

IN THE COURT OF SESSION

SUMMONS

in the cause

[*name and address*], Pursuer

against

[*name and address*], Defender

CONCLUSION

For divorce of the defender from the pursuer in respect that the marriage has broken down irretrievably by reason of the adultery of the defender.

CONDESCENDENCE

I. The pursuer resides at [*address*]. The defender resides at [*address*]. The parties are habitually resident in Scotland and have been since [*date*]. OR The parties were last habitually resident in Scotland and the [*pursuer/defender*] still resides in Scotland. OR The defender is habitually resident in Scotland and has been since [*date*]. OR The pursuer is habitually resident in Scotland and has resided in Scotland for at least a year immediately preceding the raising of this action. OR The pursuer is habitually resident in Scotland, has resided in Scotland for at least six months immediately preceding the raising of this action and is domiciled in Scotland. OR The parties are domiciled in Scotland. OR This is an action in respect of which no court of a contracting state has jurisdiction under Council Regulation (EC) No 2201/2003 and the defender is not a national of a contracting state (other than the United Kingdom or Ireland) and is not domiciled in Ireland. This court accordingly has jurisdiction. To the knowledge of the pursuer, there are no other proceedings continuing in Scotland or in any other country in respect of the marriage to which this action relates or which are **F02–02** capable of affecting its validity or subsistence.[1]

II. The parties married on [*date*] at [*place*]. An extract of the relevant entry in the register of marriages is produced herewith.

III. After the marriage, the parties lived together. In or about [*date*] the suspicions of the pursuer were aroused by the defender arriving home late at night without adequate explanation as to where he had been. On occasion the defender would stay away overnight without explanation. In or about [*date*], the pursuer challenged the defender about his behaviour when the defender admitted that he had been committing adultery with [*name*], more fully designed in the warrant for intimation. On or about [*date*] the parties separated because of the defender's ongoing adulterous association with the paramour. They have not cohabited or had marital relations with each other since then. The defender and the paramour now reside as man and wife at [*address*] where they have committed adultery. They were so resident when interviewed by private inquiry agents on or about [*date*]. The marriage has broken down irretrievably. There is no prospect of a reconciliation between the parties. The pursuer now seeks to divorce the defender.

PLEA-IN-LAW

The marriage of the parties having irretrievably broken down by reason of the defender's adultery as condescended on, decree of divorce should be granted as concluded for.

---

[1] See RCS 49.2 where such other proceedings are continuing.

Divorce—Adultery—Sheriff court

SHERIFFDOM OF [*sheriffdom*]

AT [*place*]

INITIAL WRIT

In the cause

[*name and address*], Pursuer

against

[*name and address*], Defender

The pursuer craves the court to divorce the defender from the pursuer in respect that the marriage has broken down irretrievably by reason of the adultery of the defender.

CONDESCENDENCE

I. The pursuer resides at [*address*]. The defender resides at [*address*]. The parties are habitually resident in Scotland and have been since [*date*]. *OR* The parties were last habitually resident in Scotland and the [*pursuer/defender*] still resides in Scotland. *OR* The defender is habitually resident in Scotland and has been since [*date*]. *OR* The pursuer is habitually resident in Scotland and has resided in Scotland for at least a year immediately preceding the raising of this action. *OR* The pursuer is habitually resident in Scotland, has resided in Scotland for at least six months immediately preceding the raising of this action and is domiciled in Scotland. *OR* The parties are domiciled in Scotland. *OR* This is an action in respect of which no court of a contracting state has jurisdiction under Council Regulation (EC) No 2201/2003 and the defender is not a national of a contracting state (other than the United Kingdom or Ireland) and is not domiciled in Ireland. The [*pursuer/defender*] has been resident within the sheriffdom of [*sheriffdom*] for a period of 40 days immediately preceding the raising of this action (*OR* The [*pursuer/defender*] was resident in the sheriffdom of [*sheriffdom*] for a period of not less than 40 days ending not more than

40 days before the raising of this action and has no known **F02–03**
residence in Scotland at this date.) This court accordingly
has jurisdiction. There are no other proceedings continuing in Scotland or in any other country in respect of the
marriage to which this action relates or which are capable
of affecting its validity or subsistence.[1]

II. The parties were married on [*date*] at [*place*]. An extract of
the relevant entry in the register of marriages is produced.

III. After the marriage, the parties lived together. In or about
[*date*] the suspicions of the pursuer were aroused by the
defender arriving home late at night without adequate
explanation as to where he had been. On occasion the
defender would stay away overnight without explanation.
In or about [*date*], the pursuer challenged the defender
about his behaviour when the defender admitted that he
had been committing adultery with [*name*], more fully
designed in the warrant for intimation. On or about [*date*]
the parties separated because of the defender's ongoing
adulterous association with the paramour. They have not
cohabited or had marital relations since. The defender and
the paramour now reside as man and wife at [*address*],
where they have committed adultery. They were so resident when interviewed by private inquiry agents on or
about [*date*]. The marriage has broken down irretrievably.
There is no prospect of a reconciliation between the parties. The pursuer now seeks to divorce the defender.

PLEA-IN-LAW

The marriage of the parties having irretrievably broken down
by reason of the defender's adultery as condescended on, decree
of divorce should be granted as craved.

---

[1] See OCR 33.2 where such other proceedings are continuing.

F02–04   Divorce—Non-cohabitation with consent (one year)—Court of Session

IN THE COURT OF SESSION

SUMMONS

in the cause

[*name and address*], Pursuer

against

[*name and address*], Defender

CONCLUSION

For divorce of the defender from the pursuer in respect that the marriage has broken down irretrievably by reason of non-cohabitation for one year or more and the defender's consent to decree of divorce.

CONDESCENDENCE

I. The pursuer resides at [*address*]. The defender resides at [*address*]. The parties are habitually resident in Scotland and have been since [*date*]. *OR* The parties were last habitually resident in Scotland and the [*pursuer/defender*] still resides in Scotland. *OR* The defender is habitually resident in Scotland and has been since [*date*]. *OR* The pursuer is habitually resident in Scotland and has resided in Scotland for at least a year immediately preceding the raising of this action. *OR* The pursuer is habitually resident in Scotland, has resided in Scotland for at least six months immediately preceding the raising of this action and is domiciled in Scotland. *OR* The parties are domiciled in Scotland. *OR* This is an action in respect of which no court of a contracting state has jurisdiction under Council Regulation (EC) No 2201/2003 and the defender is not a national of a contracting state (other than the United Kingdom or Ireland) and is not domiciled in Ireland. This court accordingly has jurisdiction. There are no other proceedings continuing in Scotland or in any other country in respect of the marriage to which this action **F02–04** relates or which are capable of affecting its validity or subsistence.[1]

II. The parties married on [*date*] at [*place*]. An extract of the relevant entry in the register of marriages is produced.

III. After the marriage the parties lived together until [*date*]. They then separated and have not lived with one another since. The marriage has broken down irretrievably. There is no prospect of a reconciliation between the parties. The defender consents to decree of divorce, conform to form of consent to be produced. The pursuer now seeks decree of divorce.

PLEA-IN-LAW

The marriage of the parties having irretrievably broken down by reason of non-cohabitation for a period of over one year and the defender's consent to decree of divorce, decree should be granted as concluded for.

---

[1] See RCS 49.2 where such other proceedings are continuing.

**Divorce—Non-cohabitation with consent
(one year)—Sheriff court**

SHERIFFDOM OF [*sheriffdom*]

AT [*place*]

INITIAL WRIT

In the cause

[*name and address*], Pursuer

against

[*name and address*], Defender

The pursuer craves the court to divorce the defender from the pursuer in respect that the marriage has broken down irretrievably by reason of non-cohabitation for one year or more and the defender's consent to decree of divorce.

CONDESCENDENCE

I. The pursuer resides at [*address*]. The defender resides at [*address*]. The parties are habitually resident in Scotland and have been since [*date*]. OR The parties were last habitually resident in Scotland and the [*pursuer/defender*] still resides in Scotland. OR The defender is habitually resident in Scotland and has been since [*date*]. OR The pursuer is habitually resident in Scotland and has resided in Scotland for at least a year immediately preceding the raising of this action. OR The pursuer is habitually resident in Scotland, has resided in Scotland for at least six months immediately preceding the raising of this action and is domiciled in Scotland. OR The parties are domiciled in Scotland. OR This is an action in respect of which no court of a contracting state has jurisdiction under Council Regulation (EC) No 2201/2003 and the defender is not a national of a contracting state (other than the United Kingdom or Ireland) and is not domiciled in Ireland. The [*pursuer/defender*] has been resident within the sheriffdom of [*sheriffdom*] for a period of 40 days immediately preceding the raising of this action (OR The [*pur-*

suer/defender] was resident in the sheriffdom of [*sheriffdom*]   **F02–05**
for a period of not less than 40 days ending not more than
40 days before the raising of this action and has no known
residence in Scotland at this date.) This court accordingly
has jurisdiction. There are no other proceedings continuing in Scotland or in any other country in respect of the
marriage to which this action relates or which are capable
of affecting its validity or subsistence.[1]

II. The parties were married on [*date*] at [*place*]. An extract of
the relevant entry in the register of marriages is produced.

III. After the marriage the parties lived together until [*date*].
They then separated and have not lived with one another
since. The marriage has broken down irretrievably. There
is no prospect of a reconciliation between the parties. The
defender consents to decree of divorce, conform to form of
consent to be produced. The pursuer now seeks decree of
divorce.

PLEA-IN-LAW

The marriage of the parties having irretrievably broken down
by reason of non-cohabitation for a period of over one year and
the defender's consent to decree of divorce, decree should be
granted as craved.

---

[1] See OCR 33.2 where such other proceedings are continuing.

F02–06   **Divorce—Non-cohabitation without consent (two years)—Court of Session**

IN THE COURT OF SESSION

SUMMONS

in the cause

[*name and address*], Pursuer

against

[*name and address*], Defender

CONCLUSION

For divorce of the defender from the pursuer in respect that the marriage has broken down irretrievably by reason of non-cohabitation for two years or more.

CONDESCENDENCE

I. The pursuer resides at [*address*]. The defender resides at [*address*]. The parties are habitually resident in Scotland and have been since [*date*]. OR The parties were last habitually resident in Scotland and the [*pursuer/defender*] still resides in Scotland. OR The defender is habitually resident in Scotland and has been since [*date*]. OR The pursuer is habitually resident in Scotland and has resided in Scotland for at least a year immediately preceding the raising of this action. OR The pursuer is habitually resident in Scotland, has resided in Scotland for at least six months immediately preceding the raising of this action and is domiciled in Scotland. OR The parties are domiciled in Scotland. OR This is an action in respect of which no court of a contracting state has jurisdiction under Council Regulation (EC) No 2201/2003 and the defender is not a national of a contracting state (other than the United Kingdom or Ireland) and is not domiciled in Ireland. This court accordingly has jurisdiction. There are no other proceedings continuing in Scotland or in any other country in respect of the marriage to which this action relates or which are capable of affecting its validity or **F02–06** subsistence.[1]

II. The parties married on [*date*] at [*place*]. An extract of the relevant entry in the register of marriages is produced.

III. After the marriage the parties lived together until on or about [*date*]. They then separated and have not cohabited since. The marriage has broken down irretrievably. There is no prospect of a reconciliation between the parties. The pursuer now seeks decree of divorce.

PLEA-IN-LAW

The marriage of the parties having irretrievably broken down by reason of non-cohabitation for over two years as condescended on, decree of divorce should be granted as concluded for.

---

[1] See RCS 49.2 where such other proceedings are continuing.

F02–07   Divorce—Non-cohabitation without consent (two years)—Sheriff court

SHERIFFDOM OF [*sheriffdom*]

AT [*place*]

INITIAL WRIT

In the cause

[*Name and address*]. Pursuer.

against

[*Name and address*]. Defender.

The Pursuer craves the court to divorce the defender from the pursuer in respect that the marriage has broken down irretrievably by reason of non-cohabitation for two years or more.

CONDESCENDENCE

I. The pursuer resides at [*address*]. The defender resides at [*address*]. The parties are habitually resident in Scotland and have been since [*date*]. *OR* The parties were last habitually resident in Scotland and the [*pursuer/defender*] still resides in Scotland. *OR* The defender is habitually resident in Scotland and has been since [*date*]. *OR* The pursuer is habitually resident in Scotland and has resided in Scotland for at least a year immediately preceding the raising of this action. *OR* The pursuer is habitually resident in Scotland, has resided in Scotland for at least six months immediately preceding the raising of this action and is domiciled in Scotland. *OR* The parties are domiciled in Scotland. *OR* This is an action in respect of which no court of a contracting state has jurisdiction under Council Regulation (EC) No 2201/2003 and the defender is not a national of a contracting state (other than the United Kingdom or Ireland) and is not domiciled in Ireland. The [*pursuer/defender*] has been resident within the sheriffdom of [*sheriffdom*] for a period of 40 days immediately preceding the raising of this action (*OR* The [*pursuer/defender*] was resident in the sheriffdom of [*sheriffdom*] for a period of not less than 40 days ending not more than **F02–07** 40 days before the raising of this action and has no known residence in Scotland at this date.) This court accordingly has jurisdiction. To the knowledge of the pursuer, there are no other proceedings continuing in Scotland or in any other country in respect of the marriage to which this action relates or which are capable of affecting its validity or subsistence.[1]

II. The parties were married on [*date*] at [*place*]. An extract of the relevant entry in the register of marriages is produced herewith.

III. After the marriage the parties lived together until on or about [*date*]. They then separated and have not cohabited since. The marriage has broken down irretrievably. There is no prospect of a reconciliation between the parties. The pursuer now seeks decree of divorce.

PLEA-IN-LAW

The marriage of the parties having irretrievably broken down by reason of non-cohabitation for over two years as condescended on, decree of divorce should be granted as craved.

---

[1] See OCR 33.2 where such other proceedings are continuing.

F02–08   **Divorce—Non-cohabitation without consent (two years)—Court of Session—Defender's whereabouts unknown**

IN THE COURT OF SESSION

SUMMONS

in the cause

[*name and address*], Pursuer

against

[*name and former address*] and whose current whereabouts are unknown, Defender

Warrant to intimate to [*name and address*] and [*name and address*] the children of the marriage, and to [*name and address*] the [*state relationship to defender*] as one of the next-of-kin of the defender.[1]

CONCLUSION

For divorce of the defender from the pursuer in respect that the marriage has broken down irretrievably by reason of non-cohabitation for two years or more.

CONDESCENDENCE

I. The pursuer resides at [*address*]. The defender formerly resided at [*address*]. His present whereabouts are unknown. The parties were last habitually resident in Scotland and the pursuer still resides in Scotland. OR The pursuer is habitually resident in Scotland and has resided in Scotland for at least a year immediately preceding the raising of this action. OR The pursuer is habitually resident in Scotland, has resided in Scotland for at least six months immediately preceding the raising of this action and is domiciled in Scotland. OR This is an action in respect of which no court of a contracting state has jurisdiction under Council Regulation (EC) No 2201/2003 and the defender is not a national of a contracting state (other than the United Kingdom or Ireland) and is not domiciled in Ireland. This court accordingly has jurisdiction. There are no other proceedings continuing in Scot- **F02–08** land or in any other country in respect of the marriage to which this action relates or which are capable of affecting its validity or subsistence.[2]

II. The parties married on [date] at [place]. An extract of the relevant entry in the register of marriages is produced herewith.

III. After the marriage the parties lived together until on or about [date]. As at that date, the defender left the matrimonial home. He has since refused to return and the parties have not cohabited or had marital relations since that date. The marriage has broken down irretrievably. There is no prospect of a reconciliation between the parties. The pursuer now seeks decree of divorce.

IV. The present whereabouts of the defender are unknown to the pursuer. The defender left the pursuer in the circumstances condescended upon on or about [date]. Since then, the defender has communicated only irregularly with the pursuer. The pursuer last heard from the defender on or about [date] and has no knowledge of the defender's present whereabouts. The pursuer has made enquiries of the defender's relatives and his former employers as to his whereabouts, but they have been unable to provide an address. In the circumstances the pursuer seeks warrant to intimate to [name] and [name] the children of the parties' marriage who have reached the age of 16 years, and to [name] the [state relationship to the defender] of the defender, as one of the defender's next-of-kin, each of whom is designed in the warrant for intimation.

PLEA-IN-LAW

The marriage of the parties having irretrievably broken down by reason of noncohabitation for over two years as condescended on, decree of divorce should be granted as concluded for.

IN RESPECT WHEREOF

---

[1] RCS 49.8(1)(a).
[2] See RCS 49.2 where such other proceedings are continuing.

F02–09   **Divorce—Non-cohabitation without consent (two years)—Sheriff court—Defender's whereabouts unknown**

SHERIFFDOM OF [*sheriffdom*]

AT [*place*]

INITIAL WRIT

in the cause

[*name and address*], Pursuer

against

[*name and former address*] and whose current whereabouts are unknown, Defender

The pursuer craves the court:

1. To divorce the defender from the pursuer in respect that the marriage has broken down irretrievably by reason of non-cohabitation for two years or more.

2. To grant warrant to intimate to [*name and address*] and [*name and address*] the children of the marriage, and to [*name and address*] the [*state relationship to defender*] as one of the next-of-kin of the defender.[1]

CONDESCENDENCE

I. The pursuer resides at [*address*]. The defender formerly resided at [*address*]. His present whereabouts are unknown. The parties were last habitually resident in Scotland and the pursuer still resides in Scotland. *OR* The pursuer is habitually resident in Scotland and has resided in Scotland for at least a year immediately preceding the raising of this action. *OR* The pursuer is habitually resident in Scotland, has resided in Scotland for at least six months immediately preceding the raising of this action and is domiciled in Scotland. *OR* This is an action in respect of which no court of a contracting state has jurisdiction under Council Regulation (EC) No 2201/2003

and the defender is not a national of a contracting state **F02–09**
(other than the United Kingdom or Ireland) and is not
domiciled in Ireland. The pursuer has been resident
within the sheriffdom of [*sheriffdom*] for a period of 40
days immediately preceding the raising of this action (*OR*
The pursuer was resident in the sheriffdom of [*sheriffdom*]
for a period of not less than 40 days ending not more than
40 days before the raising of this action and has no known
residence in Scotland at this date.) This court accordingly
has jurisdiction. There are no other proceedings continuing in Scotland or in any other country in respect of the
marriage to which this action relates or which are capable
of affecting its validity or subsistence.[2]

II. The parties were married on [*date*] at [*place*]. An extract of
the relevant entry in the register of marriages is produced.

III. After the marriage the parties lived together until on or
about [*date*]. As at that date, the defender left the matrimonial home. He has since refused to return and the
parties have not cohabited or had marital relations since
that date. The marriage has broken down irretrievably.
There is no prospect of a reconciliation between the parties. The pursuer now seeks decree of divorce.

IV. The present whereabouts of the defender are unknown to
the pursuer. The defender left the pursuer in the circumstances condescended upon on or about [*date*]. Since then,
the defender has communicated only irregularly with the
pursuer. The pursuer last heard from the defender on or
about [*date*] and has no knowledge of the defender's
present whereabouts. The pursuer has made enquiries of
the defender's relatives and his former employers as to his
whereabouts, but they have been unable to provide an
address. In the circumstances the pursuer seeks warrant to
intimate to [*name*] and [*name*] the children of the parties'
marriage who have reached the age of 16 years, and to
[*name*] the [*state relationship to the defender*] of the defender,
as one of the defender's next-of-kin, each of whom is
designed in the warrant for intimation.

F02–09   PLEA-IN-LAW

The marriage of the parties having irretrievably broken down
by reason of noncohabitation for over two years as condescended on, decree of divorce should be granted as craved.

IN RESPECT WHEREOF

---

[1] OCR 33.7(1)(a)
[2] See OCR 33.2 where such other proceedings are continuing.

IN THE COURT OF SESSION

SUMMONS

in the cause

[*name and address*], Pursuer

against

[*name and address*], Defender

CONCLUSION

For divorce of the defender from the pursuer in respect that the marriage has broken down irretrievably by reason of the behaviour of the defender.

CONDESCENDENCE

I. The pursuer resides at [*address*]. The defender resides at [*address*]. The parties are habitually resident in Scotland and have been since [*date*]. *OR* The parties were last habitually resident in Scotland and the [*pursuer/defender*] still resides in Scotland. *OR* The defender is habitually resident in Scotland and has been since [*date*]. *OR* The pursuer is habitually resident in Scotland and has resided in Scotland for at least a year immediately preceding the raising of this action. *OR* The pursuer is habitually resident in Scotland, has resided in Scotland for at least six months immediately preceding the raising of this action and is domiciled in Scotland. *OR* The parties are domiciled in Scotland. *OR* This is an action in respect of which no court of a contracting state has jurisdiction under Council Regulation (EC) No 2201/2003 and the defender is not a national of a contracting state (other than the United Kingdom or Ireland) and is not domiciled in Ireland. This court accordingly has jurisdiction. There are no other proceedings continuing in Scotland or in any other country in respect of the marriage to which this action

F02–10   relates or which are capable of affecting its validity or subsistence.[1]

II. The parties married on [*date*] at [*place*]. An extract of the relevant entry in the register of marriages is produced.

III. After the marriage the parties lived together. From an early stage, the marriage was unhappy because of the defender's violent and irrational behaviour. From about [*date*], the defender commenced drinking to excess. When drunk, he would be violent and abusive towards the pursuer. In particular, in or about the month of [*month*], [*year*], the defender returned home in a drunken condition and proceeded to assault the pursuer. He punched her about the face and body leaving her badly marked and shaken. The pursuer had to consult a doctor. Following upon this incident, the pursuer determined that she could no longer reside with the defender and the parties separated. They have not cohabited or had marital relations with each other since [*date*]. The pursuer can no longer reasonably be expected to cohabit with the defender. The parties' marriage has irretrievably broken down. There is no prospect of a reconciliation. The pursuer now seeks decree of divorce.

PLEA-IN-LAW

The marriage of the parties having irretrievably broken down by reason of the defender's behaviour as condescended on, decree of divorce should be granted as concluded for.

---

[1] See RCS 49.2 where such other proceedings are continuing.

Divorce—Unreasonable behaviour—Sheriff court   F02–11

SHERIFFDOM OF [*sheriffdom*]

AT [*place*]

INITIAL WRIT

In the cause

[*name and address*], Pursuer.

against

[*name and address*], Defender.

The pursuer craves the court to divorce the defender from the pursuer in respect that the marriage has broken down irretrievably by reason of the behaviour of the defender.

CONDESCENDENCE

I. The pursuer resides at [*address*]. The defender resides at [*address*]. The parties are habitually resident in Scotland and have been since [*date*]. *OR* The parties were last habitually resident in Scotland and the [*pursuer/defender*] still resides in Scotland. *OR* The defender is habitually resident in Scotland and has been since [*date*]. *OR* The pursuer is habitually resident in Scotland and has resided in Scotland for at least a year immediately preceding the raising of this action. *OR* The pursuer is habitually resident in Scotland, has resided in Scotland for at least six months immediately preceding the raising of this action and is domiciled in Scotland. *OR* The parties are domiciled in Scotland. *OR* This is an action in respect of which no court of a contracting state has jurisdiction under Council Regulation (EC) No 2201/2003 and the defender is not a national of a contracting state (other than the United Kingdom or Ireland) and is not domiciled in Ireland. The [*pursuer/defender*] has been resident within the sheriffdom of [*sheriffdom*] for a period of 40 days immediately preceding the raising of this action (*OR* The [*pursuer/defender*] was resident in the sheriffdom of [*sheriffdom*] for a period of not less than 40 days ending not more than

F02–11   40 days before the raising of this action and has no known residence in Scotland at this date.) This court accordingly has jurisdiction. There are no other proceedings continuing in Scotland or in any other country in respect of the marriage to which this action relates or which are capable of affecting its validity or subsistence.[1]

II. The parties were married on [*date*] at [*place*]. An extract of the relevant entry in the register of marriages is produced.

III. After the marriage the parties resided together. From an early stage, the marriage was unhappy due to the defender's violent and irrational behaviour. From about [*date*], the defender commenced drinking to excess. When drunk, he would be violent and abusive towards the pursuer. In particular, in or about the month of [*month*], [*year*], the defender returned home in a drunken condition and proceeded to assault the pursuer. He punched her about the face and body leaving her badly marked and shaken. The pursuer had to consult a doctor. Following upon this incident, the pursuer determined that she could no longer live with the defender and the parties separated. They have not cohabited or had marital relations with each other since [*date*]. The pursuer can no longer reasonably be expected to cohabit with the defender. The parties' marriage has irretrievably broken down. There is no prospect of a reconciliation. The pursuer now seeks decree of divorce.

PLEA-IN-LAW

The marriage of the parties having irretrievably broken down by reason of the defender's behaviour as condescended on, decree of divorce should be granted as craved.

---

[1] See OCR 33.2 where such other proceedings are continuing.

**Divorce—Unreasonable behavior—Sheriff court—Defences   F02–12
with application for a residence order**

SHERIFFDOM OF [*sheriffdom*]

AT [*place*]

DEFENCES

in the cause

[*name and address*]. Pursuer.

against

[*name and address*]. Defender.

The defender craves the court:

1. to make a residence order providing that [*name*], born
   [*date*], and [*name*], born [*date*], the children of the marriage
   under the age of 16 shall reside with the defender;

2. to grant warrant to intimate the present proceedings to
   [*name*] and [*name*], as children affected by them.

ANSWERS TO CONDESCENDENCE

I. Admitted.

II. Admitted that the parties were married at [*place*] on [*date*].
   Quoad ultra denied. Explained and averred that there are
   two children of the marriage, namely [*name*], born [*date*],
   and [*name*], born [*date*]. Extract certificates of birth are
   produced. In light of their age, dispensation of intimation
   of these proceedings upon the children is sought.

III. Admitted that after the marriage the parties lived together. Admitted that the marriage was not happy, parti-
   cularly in its later stages. Admitted that the parties
   separated in or about [*date*] and that the pursuer now
   seeks divorce. *Quoad ultra* denied except in so far as
   coinciding herewith. Explained and averred that the basic
   problem in the parties' marriage was the behaviour of the

F02–12   pursuer. From an early stage, she intimated to the defender that her career would take precedence over family life. She became increasingly uninterested in the welfare of the children and left their care to the defender. She frequently absented herself from the family home to go on excursions with colleagues from work. On occasions she was violent and abusive towards the defender. The incident condescended on, which took place in or about the month of [*month*], was caused by the pursuer's own behaviour. The defender had been out with some workmates. The pursuer was furious at having to stay at home to look after the children. When the defender returned at about [*time*], the pursuer flew at him in a rage and tried to attack him. The defender had to restrain her physically. The pursuer now cohabits with another man, whose identity is unknown to the defender.

IV. Since the separation of the parties, the children of the marriage have lived with the defender and remain in his care. He is now unemployed and able to devote his whole time to their welfare. The defender and the children remain in the former matrimonial home at [*address*]. The children are happy and well settled there. They have their own rooms, toys and friends. They attend the local school. The defender is assisted in looking after the children by his sister, Mrs [*name and address*]. The pursuer exercises informal contact with the children at weekends, but has stated that she is not interested in resuming their full time care. In the circumstances, it is in the children's best interests that the residence order craved be pronounced. In order to avoid the uncertainty that might otherwise arise over the care and residence of the children, it is better than not that such an order be made.

PLEAS-IN-LAW FOR DEFENDER

1. The marriage of the parties not having irretrievably broken down by reason of the defender's behaviour, decree of divorce should not be granted as craved.

2. It being in the best interests of the children that a residence order providing that they live with the defender should be made and it being better for them that such an order should be made than that no order be made, decree therefor should be granted as craved.

Divorce—Interim gender recognition certificate—Court of Session   F02–13

IN THE COURT OF SESSION

SUMMONS

in the cause

[*name and address*], Pursuer

against

[*name and address*], Defender

CONCLUSION

For divorce of the defender from the pursuer in respect that an interim gender recognition certificate under the Gender Recognition Act 2004 has been issued to the [*pursuer/defender*] after the date of the marriage.

CONDESCENDENCE

I. The pursuer resides at [*address*]. The defender resides at [*address*]. The parties are habitually resident in Scotland and have been since [*date*]. *OR* The parties were last habitually resident in Scotland and the [*pursuer/defender*] still resides in Scotland. *OR* The defender is habitually resident in Scotland and has been since [*date*]. *OR* The pursuer is habitually resident in Scotland and has resided in Scotland for at least a year immediately preceding the raising of this action. *OR* The pursuer is habitually resident in Scotland, has resided in Scotland for at least six months immediately preceding the raising of this action and is domiciled in Scotland. *OR* The parties are domiciled in Scotland. *OR* This is an action in respect of which no court of a contracting state has jurisdiction under Council Regulation (EC) No 2201/2003 and the defender is not a national of a contracting state (other than the United Kingdom or Ireland) and is not domiciled in Ireland. This court accordingly has jurisdiction. There are no other proceedings continuing in Scotland or in any other

F02–13   country in respect of the marriage to which this action relates or which are capable of affecting its validity or subsistence.[1]

  II. The parties married on [*date*] at [*place*]. An extract of the relevant entry in the register of marriages is produced.

  III. After the marriage an interim gender recognition certificate under the Gender Recognition Act 2004 was issued to the [*pursuer/defender*]. The interim gender recognition certificate (*OR* a certified copy of the interim gender recognition certificate) is produced herewith.[2] The pursuer now seeks decree of divorce.

PLEA-IN-LAW

An interim gender recognition certificate under the Gender Recognition Act 2004 having been issued to the [*pursuer/defender*] after the date of the marriage, decree should be granted as concluded for.

---

[1] See RCS 49.2 where such other proceedings are continuing.
[2] See RCS.49.10.

Divorce—Interim gender recognition certificate—Sheriff court F02–14

SHERIFFDOM OF [*sheriffdom*]

AT [*place*]

INITIAL WRIT

In the cause

[*name and address*]. Pursuer.

against

[*name and address*]. Defender.

The pursuer craves the court to divorce the defender from the pursuer in respect that an interim gender recognition certificate under the Gender Recognition Act 2004 has been issued to the [*pursuer/defender*] after the date of the marriage.

CONDESCENDENCE

I. The pursuer resides at [*address*]. The defender resides at [*address*]. The parties are habitually resident in Scotland and have been since [*date*]. *OR* The parties were last habitually resident in Scotland and the [*pursuer/defender*] still resides in Scotland. *OR* The defender is habitually resident in Scotland and has been since [*date*]. *OR* The pursuer is habitually resident in Scotland and has resided in Scotland for at least a year immediately preceding the raising of this action. *OR* The pursuer is habitually resident in Scotland, has resided in Scotland for at least six months immediately preceding the raising of this action and is domiciled in Scotland. *OR* The parties are domiciled in Scotland. *OR* This is an action in respect of which no court of a contracting state has jurisdiction under Council Regulation (EC) No 2201/2003 and the defender is not a national of a contracting state (other than the United Kingdom or Ireland) and is not domiciled in Ireland. The [*pursuer/defender*] has been resident within the sheriffdom of [*sheriffdom*] for a period of 40 days immediately preceding the raising of this action (*OR* The [*pursuer/defender*] was resident in the sheriffdom of [*sheriffdom*]

F02–14   for a period of not less than 40 days ending not more than 40 days before the raising of this action and has no known residence in Scotland at this date.) This court accordingly has jurisdiction. There are no other proceedings continuing in Scotland or in any other country in respect of the marriage to which this action relates or which are capable of affecting its validity or subsistence.[1]

II. The parties were married on [*date*] at [*place*]. An extract of the relevant entry in the register of marriages is produced.

III. After the marriage an interim gender recognition certificate under the Gender Recognition Act 2004 was issued to the [*pursuer/defender*]. The interim gender recognition certificate (*OR* a certified copy of the interim gender recognition certificate) is produced herewith.[2] The pursuer now seeks decree of divorce.

PLEA-IN-LAW

An interim gender recognition certificate under the Gender Recognition Act 2004 having been issued to the [*pursuer/defender*] after the date of the marriage, decree should be granted as craved.

---

[1] See OCR 33.2 where such other proceedings are continuing.
[2] See OCR 33.9A

Dissolution of civil partnership—Non-cohabitation with   F02–15
consent (one year)—Court of Session

IN THE COURT OF SESSION

SUMMONS

in the cause

[*name and address*], Pursuer

against

[*name and address*], Defender

CONCLUSION

For dissolution of the civil partnership between the pursuer and the defender in respect that the civil partnership has broken down irretrievably by reason of non-cohabitation for one year or more and the defender's consent to decree of dissolution.

CONDESCENDENCE

I. The pursuer resides at [*address*]. The defender resides at [*address*]. The parties are habitually resident in Scotland and have been since [*date*]. *OR* The parties were last habitually resident in Scotland and the [*pursuer/defender*] continues to reside in Scotland. *OR* The defender is habitually resident in Scotland and has been since [*date*]. *OR* The pursuer is habitually resident in Scotland and has resided in Scotland for at least a year immediately preceding the raising of this action. *OR* The pursuer is domiciled and habitually resident in Scotland and has resided there for at least six months immediately preceding the raising of this action. *OR* No court has, or is recognised as having, jurisdiction under the Civil Partnership (Jurisdiction and Recognition of Judgments)(Scotland) Regulations 2005 and the [*pursuer/defender*] is domiciled in Scotland at the date of the raising of this action. *OR* The parties registered as civil partners of each other in Scotland, no court has, or is recognised as having, jurisdiction under the Civil Partnership (Jurisdiction and

F02–15　Recognition of Judgments) (Scotland) Regulations 2005 and it is in the interests of justice for this court to assume jurisdiction. This court accordingly has jurisdiction. There are no other proceedings continuing in Scotland or in any other country in respect of the civil partnership to which this action relates or which are capable of affecting its validity or subsistence.[1]

II. The parties registered as civil partners of each other on [date] at [place]. An extract of the relevant entry in the civil partnership register is produced.

III. After the registration of the civil partnership the parties lived together until [date]. They then separated and have not lived with one another since. The civil partnership has broken down irretrievably. There is no prospect of a reconciliation between the parties. The defender consents to decree of dissolution of the civil partnership, conform to form of consent to be produced. The pursuer now seeks decree of dissolution.

PLEA-IN-LAW

The civil partnership between the parties having irretrievably broken down by reason of non-cohabitation for a period of over one year and the defender's consent to decree of dissolution of the civil partnership, decree should be granted as concluded for.

---

[1] See RCS 49.2 where such other proceedings are continuing.

**Dissolution of civil partnership—Non-cohabitation with   F02–16
consent (one year)—Sheriff court**

SHERIFFDOM OF [*sheriffdom*]

AT [*place*]

INITIAL WRIT

In the cause

[*name and address*]. Pursuer.

against

[*name and address*]. Defender.

The pursuer craves the court to grant decree of dissolution of the civil partnership between the pursuer and the defender in respect that the civil partnership has broken down irretrievably by reason of non-cohabitation for one year or more and the defender's consent to decree of dissolution.

CONDESCENDENCE

I. The pursuer resides at [*address*]. The defender resides at [*address*]. The parties are habitually resident in Scotland and have been since [*date*]. *OR* The parties were last habitually resident in Scotland and the [*pursuer/defender*] continues to reside in Scotland. *OR* The defender is habitually resident in Scotland and has been since [*date*]. *OR* The pursuer is habitually resident in Scotland and has resided in Scotland for at least a year immediately preceding the raising of this action. *OR* The pursuer is domiciled and habitually resident in Scotland and has resided there for at least six months immediately preceding the raising of this action. *OR* No court has, or is recognised as having, jurisdiction under the Civil Partnership (Jurisdiction and Recognition of Judgments)(Scotland) Regulations 2005 and the [*pursuer/defender*] is domiciled in Scotland at the date of the raising of this action. The [*pursuer/defender*] has been resident within the sheriffdom of [*sheriffdom*] for a period of 40 days immediately preceding the raising of this action (*OR* The [*pur-*

F02–16   *suer/defender*] was resident in the sheriffdom of [*sheriffdom*] for a period of not less than 40 days ending not more than 40 days before the raising of this action and has no known residence in Scotland at this date.) This court accordingly has jurisdiction. There are no other proceedings continuing in Scotland or in any other country in respect of the civil partnership to which this action relates or which are capable of affecting its validity or subsistence.[1]

II. The parties registered as civil partners of each other on [*date*] at [*place*]. An extract of the relevant entry in the civil partnership register is produced.

III. After the registration of the civil partnership the parties lived together until [*date*]. They then separated and have not lived with one another since. The civil partnership has broken down irretrievably. There is no prospect of a reconciliation between the parties. The defender consents to decree of dissolution of the civil partnership, conform to form of consent to be produced. The pursuer now seeks decree of dissolution.

PLEA-IN-LAW

The civil partnership between the parties having irretrievably broken down by reason of non-cohabitation for a period of over one year and the defender's consent to decree of dissolution of the civil partnership, decree should be granted as craved.

---

[1] See OCR 33A.2 where such other proceedings are continuing.

Dissolution of civil partnership—Non-cohabitation without F02–17
consent (two years)—Court of Session

IN THE COURT OF SESSION

SUMMONS

in the cause

[*name and address*], Pursuer

against

[*name and address*], Defender

CONCLUSION

For dissolution of the civil partnership between the pursuer and the defender in respect that the civil partnership has broken down irretrievably by reason of non-cohabitation for two years or more.

CONDESCENDENCE

I. The pursuer resides at [*address*]. The defender resides at [*address*]. The parties are habitually resident in Scotland and have been since [*date*]. *OR* The parties were last habitually resident in Scotland and the [*pursuer/defender*] continues to reside in Scotland. *OR* The defender is habitually resident in Scotland and has been since [*date*]. *OR* The pursuer is habitually resident in Scotland and has resided in Scotland for at least a year immediately preceding the raising of this action. *OR* The pursuer is domiciled and habitually resident in Scotland and has resided there for at least six months immediately preceding the raising of this action. *OR* No court has, or is recognised as having, jurisdiction under the Civil Partnership (Jurisdiction and Recognition of Judgments) (Scotland) Regulations 2005 and the [*pursuer/defender*] is domiciled in Scotland at the date of the raising of this action. *OR* The parties registered as civil partners of each other in Scotland, no court has, or is recognised as having, jurisdiction under the Civil Partnership (Jurisdiction and

F02–17   Recognition of Judgments) (Scotland) Regulations 2005 and it is in the interests of justice for this court to assume jurisdiction. This court accordingly has jurisdiction. There are no other proceedings continuing in Scotland or in any other country in respect of the civil partnership to which this action relates or which are capable of affecting its validity or subsistence.[1]

II. The parties registered as civil partners of each other on [*date*] at [*place*]. An extract of the relevant entry in the civil partnership register is produced.

III. After the registration of the civil partnership the parties lived together until [*date*]. They then separated and have not lived with one another since. The civil partnership has broken down irretrievably. There is no prospect of a reconciliation between the parties. The pursuer now seeks decree of dissolution.

PLEA-IN-LAW

The civil partnership between the parties having irretrievably broken down by reason of non-cohabitation for a period of over two years, decree should be granted as concluded for.

---

[1] See RCS 49.2 where such other proceedings are continuing.

**Dissolution of civil partnership—Non-cohabitation without   F02–18
consent (two years)—Sheriff court**

SHERIFFDOM OF [*sheriffdom*]

AT [*place*]

INITIAL WRIT

In the cause

[*name and address*]. Pursuer.

against

[*name and address*]. Defender.

The pursuer craves the court to grant decree of dissolution of
the civil partnership between the pursuer and the defender in
respect that the civil partnership has broken down irretrievably
by reason of non-cohabitation for two years or more.

CONDESCENDENCE

I. The pursuer resides at [*address*]. The defender resides at
[*address*]. The parties are habitually resident in Scotland
and have been since [*date*]. OR The parties were last
habitually resident in Scotland and the [*pursuer/defender*]
continues to reside in Scotland. OR The defender is
habitually resident in Scotland and has been since [*date*].
OR The pursuer is habitually resident in Scotland and has
resided in Scotland for at least a year immediately preceding the raising of this action. OR The pursuer is
domiciled and habitually resident in Scotland and has
resided there for at least six months immediately preceding the raising of this action. OR No court has, or is
recognised as having, jurisdiction under the Civil Partnership (Jurisdiction and Recognition of Judgments)
(Scotland) Regulations 2005 and the [*pursuer/defender*] is
domiciled in Scotland at the date of the raising of this
action. The [*pursuer/defender*] has been resident within the
sheriffdom of [*sheriffdom*] for a period of 40 days immediately preceding the raising of this action (OR The [*pur-
suer/defender*] was resident in the sheriffdom of [*sheriffdom*]

F02–18   for a period of not less than 40 days ending not more than 40 days before the raising of this action and has no known residence in Scotland at this date.) This court accordingly has jurisdiction. There are no other proceedings continuing in Scotland or in any other country in respect of the civil partnership to which this action relates or which are capable of affecting its validity or subsistence.[1]

II. The parties registered as civil partners of each other on [date] at [place]. An extract of the relevant entry in the civil partnership register is produced.

III. After the registration of the civil partnership the parties lived together until [date]. They then separated and have not lived with one another since. The civil partnership has broken down irretrievably. There is no prospect of a reconciliation between the parties. The pursuer now seeks decree of dissolution.

PLEA-IN-LAW

The civil partnership between the parties having irretrievably broken down by reason of non-cohabitation for a period of over two years, decree should be granted as craved.

---

[1] See OCR 33A.2 where such other proceedings are continuing.

Dissolution of civil partnership—Unreasonable   F02–19
behaviour—Court of Session

IN THE COURT OF SESSION

SUMMONS

in the cause

[*name and address*], Pursuer

against

[*name and address*], Defender

CONCLUSION

For dissolution of the civil partnership between the pursuer and the defender in respect that the civil partnership has broken down irretrievably by reason of the behaviour of the defender.

CONDESCENDENCE

I. The pursuer resides at [*address*]. The defender resides at [*address*]. The parties are habitually resident in Scotland and have been since [*date*]. *OR* The parties were last habitually resident in Scotland and the [*pursuer/defender*] continues to reside in Scotland. *OR* The defender is habitually resident in Scotland and has been since [*date*]. *OR* The pursuer is habitually resident in Scotland and has resided in Scotland for at least a year immediately preceding the raising of this action. *OR* The pursuer is domiciled and habitually resident in Scotland and has resided there for at least six months immediately preceding the raising of this action. *OR* No court has, or is recognised as having, jurisdiction under the Civil Partnership (Jurisdiction and Recognition of Judgments)(Scotland) Regulations 2005 and the [*pursuer/defender*] is domiciled in Scotland at the date of the raising of this action. *OR* The parties registered as civil partners of each other in Scotland, no court has, or is recognised as having, jurisdiction under the Civil Partnership (Jurisdiction and Recognition of Judgments)(Scotland) Regulations 2005

F02–19   and it is in the interests of justice for this court to assume jurisdiction. This court accordingly has jurisdiction. There are no other proceedings continuing in Scotland or in any other country in respect of the civil partnership to which this action relates or which are capable of affecting its validity or subsistence.[1]

II. The parties registered as civil partners of each other on [*date*] at [*place*]. An extract of the relevant entry in the civil partnership register is produced.

III. After the registration of the civil partnership the parties lived together until [*date*]. From an early stage, the civil partnership was unhappy because of the defender's violent and irrational behaviour. From about [*date*], the defender commenced drinking to excess. When drunk, he would be violent and abusive towards the pursuer. In particular, in or about the month of [*month*] [*year*], the defender returned home in a drunken condition and proceeded to assault the pursuer. He punched him about the face and body leaving him badly marked and shaken. The pursuer had to consult a doctor. Following upon this incident, the pursuer determined that he could no longer reside with the defender and the parties separated. They have not cohabited since [*date*]. The pursuer can no longer reasonably be expected to cohabit with the defender. The civil partnership has broken down irretrievably. There is no prospect of a reconciliation between the parties. The pursuer now seeks decree of dissolution.

PLEA-IN-LAW

The civil partnership between the parties having irretrievably broken down by reason of the behaviour of the defender as condescended upon, decree of dissolution should be granted as concluded for.

---

[1] See RCS 49.2 where such other proceedings are continuing.

Dissolution of civil partnership—Unreasonable behaviour—Sheriff court

SHERIFFDOM OF [*sheriffdom*]

AT [*place*]

INITIAL WRIT

In the cause

[*name and address*], Pursuer

against

[*name and address*], Defender

The pursuer craves the court to grant decree of dissolution of the civil partnership between the pursuer and the defender in respect that the civil partnership has broken down irretrievably by reason of the behaviour of the defender.

CONDESCENDENCE

I. The pursuer resides at [*address*]. The defender resides at [*address*]. The parties are habitually resident in Scotland and have been since [*date*]. OR The parties were last habitually resident in Scotland and the [*pursuer/defender*] continues to reside in Scotland. OR The defender is habitually resident in Scotland and has been since [*date*]. OR The pursuer is habitually resident in Scotland and has resided in Scotland for at least a year immediately preceding the raising of this action. OR The pursuer is domiciled and habitually resident in Scotland and has resided there for at least six months immediately preceding the raising of this action. OR No court has, or is recognised as having, jurisdiction under the Civil Partnership (Jurisdiction and Recognition of Judgments)(Scotland) Regulations 2005 and the [*pursuer/defender*] is domiciled in Scotland at the date of the raising of this action. The [*pursuer/defender*] has been resident within the sheriffdom of [*sheriffdom*] for a period of 40 days immediately preceding the raising of this action (OR The [*pursuer/defender*] was resident in the sheriffdom of [*sheriffdom*]

F02–20   for a period of not less than 40 days ending not more than 40 days before the raising of this action and has no known residence in Scotland at this date.) This court accordingly has jurisdiction. There are no other proceedings continuing in Scotland or in any other country in respect of the civil partnership to which this action relates or which are capable of affecting its validity or subsistence.[1]

II. The parties registered as civil partners of each other on [*date*] at [*place*]. An extract of the relevant entry in the civil partnership register is produced.

III. After the registration of the civil partnership the parties lived together until [*date*]. From an early stage, the civil partnership was unhappy due to the defender's violent and irrational behaviour. From about [*date*], the defender commenced drinking to excess. When drunk, she would be violent and abusive towards the pursuer. In particular, in or about the month of [*date*] [*year*], the defender returned home in a drunken condition and proceeded to assault the pursuer. She punched her about the face and body leaving her badly marked and shaken. The pursuer had to consult a doctor. Following upon this incident, the pursuer determined that she could no longer reside with the defender and the parties separated. They have not cohabited since [*date*]. The pursuer can no longer reasonably be expected to cohabit with the defender. The civil partnership has broken down irretrievably. There is no prospect of a reconciliation between the parties. The pursuer now seeks decree of dissolution.

PLEA-IN-LAW

The civil partnership between the parties having irretrievably broken down by reason of the behaviour of the defender as condescended upon, decree of dissolution should be granted as craved.

---

[1] See OCR 33A.2 where such other proceedings are continuing.

**Dissolution of civil partnership—Interim gender recognition   F02–21
certificate—Court of Session**

IN THE COURT OF SESSION

SUMMONS

in the cause

[*name and address*], Pursuer

against

[*name and address*], Defender

CONCLUSION

For dissolution of the civil partnership between the pursuer and
the defender in respect that an interim gender recognition certificate under the Gender Recognition Act 2004 has been issued
to the [*pursuer/defender*] after the date of the registration of the
civil partnership.

CONDESCENDENCE

I. The pursuer resides at [*address*]. The defender resides at
[*address*]. The parties are habitually resident in Scotland
and have been since [*date*]. *OR* The parties were last
habitually resident in Scotland and the [pursuer/defen-
der] continues to reside in Scotland. *OR* The defender is
habitually resident in Scotland and has been since [*date*].
OR The pursuer is habitually resident in Scotland and has
resided in Scotland for at least a year immediately preceding the raising of this action. *OR* The pursuer is
domiciled and habitually resident in Scotland and has
resided there for at least six months immediately preceding the raising of this action. *OR* No court has, or is
recognised as having, jurisdiction under the Civil Partnership (Jurisdiction and Recognition of Judgments)
(Scotland) Regulations 2005 and the [*pursuer/defender*] is
domiciled in Scotland at the date of the raising of this
action. *OR* The parties registered as civil partners of each
other in Scotland, no court has, or is recognised as having,

F02–21   jurisdiction under the Civil Partnership (Jurisdiction and
Recognition of Judgments) (Scotland) Regulations 2005
and it is in the interests of justice for this court to assume
jurisdiction. This court accordingly has jurisdiction. There
are no other proceedings continuing in Scotland or in any
other country in respect of the civil partnership to which
this action relates or which are capable of affecting its
validity or subsistence.[1]

II. The parties registered as civil partners of each other on
[*date*] at [*place*]. An extract of the relevant entry in the civil
partnership register is produced.

III. After the registration of the civil partnership an interim
gender recognition certificate under the Gender Recognition Act 2004 was issued to the [*pursuer/defender*]. The
interim gender recognition certificate (*OR* a certified copy
of the interim gender recognition certificate) is produced
herewith.[2] The pursuer now seeks decree of dissolution of
the civil partnership.

PLEA-IN-LAW

An interim gender recognition certificate under the Gender
Recognition Act 2004 having been issued to the [*pursuer/defen-
der*] after the date of the registration of the civil partnership,
decree of dissolution should be granted as concluded for.

---

[1] See RCS 49.2 where such other proceedings are continuing.
[2] See RCS 49.10.

Dissolution of civil partnership—Interim gender recognition **F02–22**
certificate—Sheriff court

SHERIFFDOM OF [*sheriffdom*]

AT [*place*]

INITIAL WRIT

In the cause

[*name and address*], Pursuer.

against

[*name and address*], Defender.

The pursuer craves the court to grant decree of dissolution of the civil partnership between the pursuer and the defender in respect that an interim gender recognition certificate under the Gender Recognition Act 2004 has been issued to the [*pursuer/ defender*] after the date of the registration of the civil partnership.

CONDESCENDENCE

I. The pursuer resides at [*address*]. The defender resides at [*address*]. The parties are habitually resident in Scotland and have been since [*date*]. *OR* The parties were last habitually resident in Scotland and the [*pursuer/defender*] continues to reside in Scotland. *OR* The defender is habitually resident in Scotland and has been since [*date*]. *OR* The pursuer is habitually resident in Scotland and has resided in Scotland for at least a year immediately preceding the raising of this action. *OR* The pursuer is domiciled and habitually resident in Scotland and has resided there for at least six months immediately preceding the raising of this action. *OR* No court has, or is recognised as having, jurisdiction under the Civil Partnership (Jurisdiction and Recognition of Judgments)(Scotland) Regulations 2005 and the [*pursuer/defender*] is domiciled in Scotland at the date of the raising of this action. The [*pursuer/defender*] has been resident within the sheriffdom of [*sheriffdom*] for a period of 40 days immediately preceding the raising of this action (*OR* The

F02–22   [*pursuer/defender*] was resident in the sheriffdom of [*sheriffdom*] for a period of not less than 40 days ending not more than 40 days before the raising of this action and has no known residence in Scotland at this date.) This court accordingly has jurisdiction. There are no other proceedings continuing in Scotland or in any other country in respect of the civil partnership to which this action relates or which are capable of affecting its validity or subsistence.[1]

    II. The parties registered as civil partners of each other on [*date*] at [*place*]. An extract of the relevant entry in the civil partnership register is produced.

    III. After the registration of the civil partnership an interim gender recognition certificate under the Gender Recognition Act 2004 was issued to the [pursuer/defender]. The interim gender recognition certificate (*OR* a certified copy of the interim gender recognition certificate) is produced herewith.[2] The pursuer now seeks decree of dissolution of the civil partnership.

PLEA-IN-LAW

An interim gender recognition certificate under the Gender Recognition Act 2004 having been issued to the [pursuer/defender] after the date of the registration of the civil partnership, decree of dissolution should be granted as craved.

---

[1] See OCR 33A.2 where such other proceedings are continuing.
[2] See OCR 33A.9.

Incidental elements—Minute for decree in undefended actions[1]

F02–23

[*Name*], [agent/counsel for the pursuer], having considered the evidence contained in the affidavits and the other documents as specified in the attached schedule and being satisfied that on this evidence a motion for decree in terms of the conclusions of the summons (*OR* in terms of the craves of the initial writ) [*or in such restricted terms as may be appropriate*] may properly be made, moves the court accordingly.

IN RESPECT WHEREOF

SCHEDULE

1. Marriage (*OR* civil partnership) certificate of parties.

2. Affidavit of pursuer.

3. Affidavit of supporting witness.

4. (Other productions as are appropriate).

---

[1] RCS 49.29; OCR 33.29, OCR 33A.30.

Separation

Actions for separation are still competent in both the Court of Session and the sheriff court. They proceed upon the same grounds as are available for actions of divorce or dissolution of civil partnership. Thus, actions of separation may be brought on the ground of the defender's behaviour, non-cohabitation for a period of one year or more with the defender's consent to the granting of decree of separation, non-cohabitation for a period of two years or more, the defender's adultery (married couples only) and the issuing of an interim gender recognition certificate under the Gender Recognition Act 2004 to either party since the date of the marriage or registration of the civil partnership.

Actions of separation are of little practical purpose. Clive, in the fourth edition of his *Law of Husband and Wife in Scotland* at p.361, describes them as being "something of an absurdity". He points out that the Scottish Law Commission has suggested that judicial separation should be abolished.

If it is desired to bring an action for separation, the relative conclusion/crave, articles of condescendence and pleas-in-law will closely follow those already given in the divorce and dissolution of civil partnership section, with the substitution of the remedy of separation for that of divorce or dissolution.

FINANCIAL PROVISION

To grant warrant to intimate to [*name and address*] as a person the consent of whom is required in respect of the order for transfer of title sought in the [*number*] crave.

To grant warrant to intimate to [*name and address*] as the person in whose favour the transfer of [*or* transaction involving] property referred to in the condescendence of this writ was made [*or* is to be made] [*or* as a person having an interest in the transfer of/transaction involving property referred to in the condescendence of this writ].

To [grant warrant to] intimate to [*name and address*] as trustees [*or* managers] of the pension scheme in respect of which an order is sought in [the [*number*] conclusion of this summons] [[*number*] crave hereof].

To [grant warrant to] intimate to [*name and address*] as a person who is believed to be a creditor of [*name of party*] in respect of the property sought to be transferred in [the [*number*] conclusion of this summons] [[*number*] crave hereof].

F03–02   **Aliment[1]—Additional—Court of Session**

IN THE COURT OF SESSION

SUMMONS

in the cause

[*name and address*], pursuer

against

[*name and address*], defender

CONCLUSION

For payment by the defender to the pursuer of [*amount of sum in words*] £[*figures*] per [*week/month*] as aliment for each child, payable in advance and with interest thereon at the rate of eight per cent a year on each [*weekly/monthly*] payment from the due date until payment.

CONDESCENDENCE

I. (Take in jurisdiction style for divorce or dissolution of civil partnership if appropriate *OR* jurisdiction may be based on defender's domicile or habitual residence.[2] In either case add at the end an averment about any maintenance orders within the meaning of section 106 of the Debtors (Scotland) Act 1987.[3])

II. The parties separated on or about [*date*]. Since then the two children of the relationship have remained in the care of the pursuer. The pursuer is presently entitled to the amounts provided for in the maintenance calculation made under section 11 of the Child Support Act 1991. On [*date*] the defender was ordered to pay the sum of £[*amount in figures*] per week for the two children.[4] That calculation was made on the basis that the defender is in employment as [*job title*] at a monthly salary of £[*amount in figures*]. The defender has an interest in a company named [*name*] and receives a salary of £[*amount in figures*] per month therefrom. In addition he has a substantial private

income of approximately £[*amount in figures*] from various **F03–02**
investments. When the parties were living together the
children enjoyed a comfortable lifestyle financed by the
defender. [*Add further specification as appropriate.*][5] In the
circumstances the pursuer seeks an award of aliment for
each of the children at the rate of £[*amount in figures*] per
[*week/month*] in addition to the amount the defender pays
in terms of the Child Support Act calculation. The pursuer
is unemployed and dependent on contributions made by
the defender for aliment of the children. It is accordingly
appropriate that an additional award of aliment is made.

PLEA-IN-LAW

In the circumstances condescended upon, it being appropriate
that the defender should pay the additional aliment sought for
the children, decree therefor should be pronounced as concluded for.[6]

---

[1] The jurisdiction of the court to award aliment has largely been ousted by
the Child Support Act 1991. The court has certain limited areas of jurisdiction
still remaining: see s.8 of the 1991 Act and Wilkinson and Norrie, *Parent and
Child*, 2nd edn, pp.449–450.
[2] Civil Jurisdiction and Judgments Act 1982.
[3] RCS 49.5.
[4] RCS 49.6(2)(a).
[5] These averments relate to circumstances where an additional award in
terms of s.8(6) is sought. Where appropriate, averments in support of s.8(7), (8)
and (10) should be substituted.
[6] This plea-in-law relates to an additional award in terms of s.8(6). It should
be adapted where aliment is sought in terms of s.8(7), (8) or (10).

F03–03 **Aliment[1]—Additional—Sheriff court**

SHERIFFDOM OF [*sheriffdom*]

AT [*place*]

INITIAL WRIT

in the cause

[*name and address*], Pursuer

against

[*name and address*], Defender

The pursuer craves the court to grant decree for payment by the defender to the pursuer of [*amount of sum in words*] £[*figures*] per [*week/month*] as aliment for each child, payable in advance and with interest thereon at the rate of eight per cent a year on each [*weekly/monthly*] payment from the due date until payment.

CONDESCENDENCE

I. (Take in jurisdiction style for divorce or dissolution of civil partnership if appropriate *OR* jurisdiction may be based on defender's domicile or habitual residence[2]. In either case add at the end an averment about any maintenance orders within the meaning of section 106 of the Debtors (Scotland) Act 1987.[3])

II. The parties separated on or about [*date*]. Since then the two children of the relationship have remained in the care of the pursuer. The pursuer is presently entitled to the amounts provided for in the maintenance calculation made under section 11 of the Child Support Act 1991. On [*date*] the defender was ordered to pay the sum of £[*amount in figures*] per week for the two children[4]. That calculation was made on the basis that the defender is in employment as [*job title*] at a monthly salary of £[*amount in figures*]. The defender has an interest in a company named [*name*] and receives a salary of £[*amount in figures*] per month therefrom. In addition he has a substantial private income of approximately £[*amount in figures*] from various

investments. When the parties were living together the **F03–03**
children enjoyed a comfortable lifestyle financed by the
defender. [*Add further specification as appropriate.*][5] In the
circumstances the pursuer seeks an award of aliment for
each of the children at the rate of £[*amount in figures*] per
[*week/month*] in addition to the amount the defender pays
in terms of the Child Support Act calculation. The pursuer
is unemployed and totally dependent on contributions
made by the defender for aliment of said children. It is
accordingly appropriate that an additional award of aliment is made.

PLEA-IN-LAW

In the circumstances condescended upon, it being appropriate
that the defender should pay the additional aliment sought for
the children, decree therefor should be pronounced as craved.[6]

---

[1] The jurisdiction of the court to award aliment has largely been ousted by
the Child Support Act 1991. The court has certain limited areas of jurisdiction
still remaining: see s.8 of the 1991 Act and Wilkinson and Norrie, *Parent and
Child*, 2nd edn, pp.449–450.
[2] Civil Jurisdiction and Judgments Act 1982.
[3] OCR 33.5, 33A.5.
[4] OCR 33.6(2), 33A.6(2).
[5] These averments relate to circumstances where an additional award in
terms of section 8(6) is sought. Where appropriate, averments in support of
section 8(7), (8) and (10) should be substituted.
[6] This plea-in-law relates to an additional award in terms of s.8(6). It should
be adapted where aliment is sought in terms of s.8(7), (8) or (10).

      Aliment—Child over 18—Court of Session

IN THE COURT OF SESSION

SUMMONS

in the cause

[*name and address*], Pursuer

against

[*name and address*], Defender

CONCLUSION

For payment by the defender to the pursuer of [*amount of sum in words*] £[*figures*] per [*week/month*] as aliment for the pursuer, payable in advance and with interest thereon at the rate of eight per cent a year on each [*weekly/monthly*] payment from the due date until payment.

CONDESCENDENCE

I. The pursuer resides at [*address*]. The defender resides at [*address*]. He is domiciled (*OR* habitually resident) there[1]. This court accordingly has jurisdiction. No maintenance order (within the meaning of section 106 of the Debtors (Scotland) Act 1987) has been granted in favour of or against the pursuer.[2]

II. The pursuer is the son of the defender. He is 20 years of age. His date of birth is [*date*]. He is presently in full time education as a student at [*name of university or college*]. Until his nineteenth birthday the pursuer was entitled to a monthly payment of £[*amount in figures*] from the defender in terms of a maintenance calculation made under the Child Support Act 1991. The defender has now declined to make any further payment to aliment the pursuer. The pursuer has no income of his own except holiday earnings and his student loan which are expended on his day-to-day living expenses. He has no other means of support. The defender is in employment as [*job title*] at an

approximate salary of £[*amount in figures*]. He is able to **F03–04**
afford the sum of aliment sought. The sum sought by the
pursuer is reasonable in the circumstances. He lives at
home with his mother from whom the defender is separated. She is not in employment and is dependent on State
benefits.

PLEA-IN-LAW

The defender having an obligation to aliment the pursuer and
the sum sought being reasonable, decree therefor should be
granted as concluded for.

---

[1] Civil Jurisdiction and Judgments Act 1982.
[2] RCS 49.5.

F03–05   Aliment—Child over 18—Sheriff court

SHERIFFDOM OF [*sheriffdom*] AT [*place*]

INITIAL WRIT

in the cause

[*name and address*], Pursuer

against

[*name and address*], Defender

The pursuer craves the court to grant decree for payment by the defender to the pursuer of [*amount of sum in words*] £[*figures*] per [*week/month*] as aliment for the pursuer, payable in advance and with interest thereon at the rate of eight per cent a year on each [*weekly/monthly*] payment from the due date until payment.

CONDESCENDENCE

I. The pursuer resides at [*address*]. The defender resides at [*address*]. He is domiciled (*OR* habitually resident) there[1]. This court accordingly has jurisdiction. No maintenance order (within the meaning of section 106 of the Debtors (Scotland) Act 1987) has been granted in favour of or against the pursuer.[2])

II. The pursuer is the son of the defender. He is 20 years of age. His date of birth is [*date*]. He is presently in full time education as a student at [*name of university or college*]. Until his nineteenth birthday the pursuer was entitled to a monthly payment of £[*amount in figures*] from the defender in terms of a maintenance calculation made under the Child Support Act 1991. The defender has now declined to make any further payment to aliment the pursuer. The pursuer has no income of his own except holiday earnings and his student loan which are expended on his day-to-day living expenses. He has no other means of support. The defender is in employment as [*job title*] at an approximate salary of £[*amount in figures*]. He is able to afford the sum of aliment sought. The sum sought by the pursuer is reasonable in the circumstances. He lives at

home with his mother from whom the defender is sepa- **F03–05**
rated. She is not in employment and is dependent on State
benefits.

PLEA-IN-LAW

The defender having an obligation to aliment the pursuer and
the sum sought being reasonable, decree therefor should be
granted as craved.

---

[1] Civil Jurisdiction and Judgments Act 1982.
[2] OCR 33.5.

F03–06   **Capital sum—Transfer of title—Periodical allowance—Interim aliment—Court of Session**

IN THE COURT OF SESSION

SUMMONS

in the cause

[*name and address*], Pursuer

against

[*name and address*], Defender

CONCLUSIONS

FIRST   For payment by the defender to the pursuer of a capital sum of [*words*] (£[*figures*]) with interest thereon at the rate of eight per cent a year from the date of decree to follow hereon until payment.

OR

FIRST   For payment by the defender to the pursuer of a capital sum of [*words*] (£[*figures*]) with interest thereon at the rate of eight per cent a year from [*date of separation/date of citation*] or from such other date as the court considers appropriate until payment.

SECOND   For the transfer of the defender's whole right, title and interest in and to the heritable property known as and forming [*address*], together with the furniture and plenishings contained therein to the pursuer; to ordain the defender to make, execute and deliver to the pursuer a valid disposition of the defender's right title and interest to the property and such other deeds as may be necessary to give the pursuer a valid title to the property and the furniture and plenishings, and that within one month of the date of decree to follow hereon; and in the event of the defender failing to make, execute and deliver such disposition and other deeds, to authorise and ordain the Deputy Principal Clerk of Session to

subscribe on behalf of the defender a disposition of **F03–06**
the said heritable property as adjusted at the sight
of the Deputy Principal Clerk of Session together
with such other deeds as may be necessary to give
the pursuer a valid title to the property and the
furniture and plenishings.

THIRD   For payment by the defender to the pursuer of a
periodical allowance of [*words*] (£[*figures*]) per [*week/
month*] payable [*weekly/monthly*] in advance until
the death or remarriage (*OR* registration of a new
civil partnership) of the pursuer or for such other
period as the court shall consider appropriate with
interest thereon at the rate of eight per cent a year
on each [*weekly/monthly*] payment from the date the
same falls due until it is paid.

OR

THIRD   For payment by the defender to the pursuer of a
periodical allowance of [*words*] (£[*figures*]) per [*week/
month*] for a period of three years from the date of
decree to follow hereon or for such other period as
the court shall consider appropriate with interest
thereon at the rate of eight per cent a year on each
[*weekly/monthly*] payment from the date the same
falls due until it is paid; and for interim aliment at
said rate.

CONDESCENDENCE

I. (Take in jurisdiction style for divorce or dissolution of civil
partnership. Add at the end an averment about any
maintenance orders within the meaning of s.106 of the
Debtors (Scotland) Act 1987.[1] Add articles giving the
details of the marriage (*OR* partnership) and grounds of
divorce (*OR* dissolution of partnership).)

II. The matrimonial (*OR* partnership) property includes:
   (i)   the *family home* at [*address*], with a value at the rele-
        vant date of £[*figure*];
  (ii)   the furniture and plenishings in the family home,
        valued at approximately £[*figure*] at the relevant date;
 (iii)   the defender's Army pension with a CETV at the

relevant date of £[*figure*], of which £[*figure*] is referable to the period of the marriage [*OR* partnership];
  (iv) the parties' joint bank account with the Royal Bank of Scotland, account number [*specify*] which had a balance of £[*figures*] at the relevant date;
  (v) the defender's Standard Life policy number [*specify*] with a value of £[*figure*] at the relevant date;
  (vi) Volvo registration number [*specify*] registered in the pursuer's name with a relevant date value of about £[*figure*].
  The parties' liabilities comprise:
  (a) standard security in favour of the Royal Bank of Scotland in the sum of £[*figure*];
  (b) car loan in the sum of £[*figure*].
  The pursuer seeks a fair share of the matrimonial (*OR* partnership) property. The pursuer has made a substantial non-financial contribution throughout the marriage (*OR* partnership) by staying at home, attending to all household duties and caring for the children. She is now disadvantaged on the labour market as a result of her contributions. The defender has gained the advantage of being able to pursue a career while the defender's domestic needs have been catered for and the children looked after by the pursuer. The pursuer has been entirely dependent upon the defender for financial support throughout the parties' marriage (*OR* partnership). She has no real prospect of obtaining full time employment. She would suffer grave financial hardship if she ceased to be entitled to alimentary provision from the defender as a result of the divorce (*OR* dissolution of the civil partnership). In all the circumstances the orders sought for transfer of the defender's right, title and interest in the property to the pursuer, payment of a capital sum and of periodical allowance are justified and reasonable.

III. The pursuer is not in employment. She qualified as a [*job title*] before giving up work to bring up the parties' children. She presently has no means of support and is reliant upon voluntary payments of aliment by the defender of £[*amount in figures*] per month. These payments are insufficient for her needs. The pursuer's outgoings in respect of herself, the children and the family home amount to £[*amount in figures*] per month. The defender is a [*job title*] and earns in excess of £[*amount in figures*] per annum. In the circumstances the sum sought in respect of aliment and by way of periodical allowance is reasonable.

PLEAS-IN-LAW

1. The order sought for payment of a capital sum being justified in terms of s.9(1)(a) and (b) of the Family Law (Scotland) Act of 1985 and reasonable having regard to the parties' resources should be granted as concluded for.

2. The order for the transfer to the pursuer of the defender's right, title and interest in the family home and the furniture and plenishings therein being justified in terms of s.9(1)(a), (b) and (c) of the said Act of 1985 and reasonable having regard to the parties' resources, decree therefor should be granted as concluded for.

3. The order sought for payment of a periodical allowance being justified by the principles in s.9(1)(d) and (e) of the said Act of 1985 and reasonable having regard to the parties' resources, and an order for payment of a capital sum and transfer of property being insufficient to satisfy the requirements of s.8(2) of the said Act, the order concluded for should be granted.

4. The sum sued for by way of interim aliment being reasonable decree therefor should be granted as concluded for.

---

[1] RCS 49.5.

F03–07   **Capital sum—Transfer of title—Periodical allowance—Interim aliment—Sheriff court**

SHERIFFDOM OF [*sheriffdom*]

AT [*place*]

INITIAL WRIT

in the cause

[*name and address*], pursuer

against

[*name and address*], defender

The pursuer craves the court:

(1) To grant decree for payment by the defender to the pursuer of a capital sum of [*words*] (£[*figures*]) with interest thereon at the rate of eight per cent a year from the date of decree to follow hereon until payment.

OR

(1) To grant decree for payment by the defender to the pursuer of a capital sum of [*words*] (£[*figures*]) with interest thereon at the rate of eight per cent a year from [*date of separation/date of citation*] or from such other date as the court considers appropriate until payment.

(2) To grant decree for the transfer of the defender's whole right, title and interest in and to the heritable property known as and forming [*address*], together with the furniture and plenishings contained therein to the pursuer; to ordain the defender to make, execute and deliver to the pursuer a valid disposition of the defender's right, title and interest to the property and such other deeds as may be necessary to give the pursuer a valid title to the property and to the furniture and plenishings and that within one month of the date of decree to follow hereon and in the event of the defender failing to make, execute and deliver such disposition and other deeds to authorise and ordain the sheriff clerk to subscribe on behalf of the

defender a disposition of the heritable property as adjus- **F03–07**
ted at the sight of the sheriff clerk together with such other
deeds as may be necessary to give the pursuer a valid title
to the heritable property and to the furniture and plenishings.

(3) To grant decree against the defender for payment to the
pursuer of a periodical allowance of [*words*] (£[*figures*]) per
[*week/month*] payable [*weekly/monthly*] in advance until the
death or remarriage (*OR* registration of a new civil partnership) of the pursuer or for such other period as the
court shall consider appropriate with interest thereon at
the rate of eight per cent a year on each [*weekly/monthly*]
payment from the date the same falls due until it is paid.

OR

(3) To grant decree against the defender for payment to the
pursuer of a periodical allowance of [*words*] (£[*figures*]) per
[*week/month*] for a period of three years from the date of
decree to follow hereon or for such other period as the
court shall consider appropriate with interest thereon at
the rate of eight per cent a year on each [*weekly/monthly*]
payment from the date the same falls due until it is paid;
and for interim aliment at said rate.

CONDESCENDENCE

I. (Take in jurisdiction style for divorce or dissolution of civil
partnership. Add at the end an averment about any
maintenance orders within the meaning of section 106 of
the Debtors (Scotland) Act 1987.[1] Add articles giving the
details of the marriage (*OR* partnership) and grounds of
divorce (*OR* dissolution of partnership).)

II. The matrimonial (*OR* partnership) property includes:
   (i)   the *family home* at [*address*], with a value at the rele-
         vant date of £[*figure*];
   (ii) the furniture and plenishings in the family home,
         valued at approximately £[*figure*] at the relevant date;
   (iii) the defender's Army pension with a CETV at the
         relevant date of £[*figure*], of which £[*figure*] is refer-
         able to the period of the marriage [*OR* partnership];
   (iv) the parties' joint bank account with the Royal Bank of

F03–07   Scotland, account number [*specify*] which had a balance of £[*figures*] at the relevant date;

(v)   the defender's Standard Life policy number [*specify*] with a value of £[*figure*] at the relevant date;

(vi) Volvo registration number [*specify*] registered in the pursuer's name with a relevant date value of about £[*figure*].

The parties' liabilities comprise:

(a)   standard security in favour of the Royal Bank of Scotland in the sum of £[*figure*];

(b)   car loan in the sum of £[*figure*].

The pursuer seeks a fair share of the matrimonial (*OR* partnership) property. The pursuer has made a substantial non-financial contribution throughout the marriage (*OR* partnership) by staying at home, attending to all household duties and caring for the children. She is now disadvantaged on the labour market as a result of her contributions. The defender has gained the advantage of being able to pursue a career while the defender's domestic needs have been catered for and the children looked after by the pursuer. The pursuer has been entirely dependent upon the defender for financial support throughout the parties' marriage (*OR* partnership). She has no real prospect of obtaining full time employment. She would suffer grave financial hardship if she ceased to be entitled to financial provision from the defender as a result of the divorce (*OR* dissolution of the civil partnership). In all the circumstances the orders sought for transfer of the defender's right, title and interest in the property to the pursuer, payment of a capital sum and of periodical allowance are justified and reasonable.

III. The pursuer is not in employment. She qualified as a [*job title*] before giving up work to bring up the parties' children. She has no means of support and is reliant upon aliment from the defender of £[*amount in figures*] per month. These payments are insufficient for her needs. The pursuer's outgoings in respect of herself, the children and the family home amount to £[*amount in figures*] per month. The defender is a [*job title*] and earns in excess of £[*amount in figures*] per annum. In the circumstances the sum sought in respect of periodical allowance is reasonable.

PLEAS-IN-LAW

1. The order sought for payment of a capital sum being justified in terms of s.9(1)(a) and (b) of the Family Law (Scotland) Act of 1985 and reasonable having regard to the parties' resources should be granted as craved.

2. The order for the transfer to the pursuer of the defender's right, title and interest in the family home and the furniture and plenishings therein being justified in terms of s.9(1)(a), (b) and (c) of the said Act of 1985 and reasonable having regard to the parties' resources, decree therefor should be granted as craved.

3. The order sought for payment of a periodical allowance being justified by the principles in s.9(1)(d) and (e) of the said Act of 1985 and reasonable having regard to theparties' resources, and an order for payment of a capital sum and transfer of property being insufficient to satisfy the requirements of section 8(2) of the said Act, decree therefor should be granted as craved.

4. The sum sued for by way of interim aliment reasonable decree therefor should be granted as craved.

---

[1] OCR 33.5 and 33A.5.

F03–08 Pensions—Order in terms of section 12A of the Family Law (Scotland) Act 1985—(In conjunction with conclusion for capital sum) Conclusion and supporting averments—Court of Session

IN THE COURT OF SESSION

SUMMONS

in the cause

[*name, designation and address*], Pursuer

Against

[*name, designation and address*], Defender

CONCLUSION

For an order directing [*name and address*] as trustees of the [*name of pension scheme*] to pay to the pursuer the lump sum due to be paid to the defender in terms of said scheme on [*dates*] or his earlier retiral.

CONDESCENDENCE

[*Insert details of other relevant matrimonial property, etc.*]
The defender has accumulated an interest in an occupational pension scheme with [*name of employers*] during the course of the marriage. The said scheme is administered by [*name and address of trustees*]. The defender is aged [*age*]. He will retire on [*date*]. On that date he will receive a lump sum payment of about £[*amount*] as part of his pension provision at that time. A statement of benefits relating to the defender's said pension is produced. In these circumstances, in addition to the other orders sought, the pursuer seeks payment to her of the lump sum which will be payable to the defender on the said date. The order sought is justified in the circumstances.

PLEA-IN-LAW

There being circumstances to justify an order directing the said trustees of the defender's occupational pension scheme to make

payment of the lump sum due to him on [*date*] direct to the **F03–08**
pursuer and such payment being reasonable having regard to
the parties' resources, an order in terms of section 12A(2) of the
said Act of 1985 should be made accordingly.

F03–09 Pensions—Order in terms of section 12A of the Family Law (Scotland) Act 1985—(In conjunction with conclusion for capital sum) Conclusion and supporting averments—Sheriff court

INITIAL WRIT

SHERIFFDOM OF [*sheriffdom*]
AT [*place*]

[*name, designation and address*]. Pursuer.

Against

[*name, designation and address*]. Defender.

The pursuer craves the court for an order directing [*name and address*] as trustees of the [*name of pension scheme*] to pay to the pursuer the lump sum due to be paid to the defender in terms of said scheme on [*dates*] or his earlier retiral.

CONDESCENDENCE

[*Insert details of other relevant matrimonial property, etc.*]
The defender has accumulated an interest in an occupational pension scheme with [*name of employers*] during the course of the marriage. The said scheme is administered by [*name and address of trustees*]. The defender is aged [*age*]. He will retire on [*date*]. On that date he will receive a lump sum payment of about £[*amount*] as part of his pension provision at that time. A statement of benefits relating to the defender's said pension is produced. In these circumstances, in addition to the other orders sought, the pursuer seeks payment to her of the lump sum which will be payable to the defender on the said date. The order sought is justified in the circumstances.

PLEA-IN-LAW

There being circumstances to justify an order directing the said trustees of the defender's occupational pension scheme to make payment of the lump sum due to him on [*date*] direct to the pursuer and such payment being reasonable having regard to the parties' resources, an order in terms of section 12A(2) of the said Act of 1985 should be made accordingly.

Pension Sharing Order—Conclusion and supporting averments—Court of Session

IN THE COURT OF SESSION

SUMMONS

in the cause

[*name and address*], pursuer

against

[*name and address*], defender

Warrant for intimation to [*name and address of the administrators of the relevant pension scheme: see RCS 49.8(1)(l)*].

CONCLUSION

For a pension sharing order providing that the defender's shareable pension rights in the [*scheme*] be subject to pension sharing for the benefit of the pursuer and that the sum of £[*amount*] with interest accrued at the rate of eight per cent a year from [*date of separation*] until the date of transfer of the appropriate pension credit into a qualifying scheme for the pursuer be so transferred.

CONDESCENDENCE

[*Take in Articles of Condescendence of other divorce/dissolution of civil partnership actions*]

The most substantial undivided matrimonial (*OR* partnership) asset is the defender's pension. The defender retired on [*date*]. The defender's date of birth is [*date*]. The pursuer was born on [*date*]. The pursuer was financially dependent on the defender throughout the parties' marriage (*OR* civil partnership). The pursuer made substantial non-financial contributions to the defender and the parties' children during the years when the defender was in employment. The pursuer ran the family home and brought up the children. The pursuer is economically disadvantaged as a result. The pursuer has no personal pension

F03–10 provision. *He/she* will require to provide *himself/herself* with an income for the rest of *his/her* life. The defender's pension is shareable. In the circumstances the order sought for a pension sharing order in terms of which a sum representing 50 per cent of the value of the defender's pension at the date of separation is to be transferred to the pursuer is justified and reasonable.

PLEA-IN-LAW

[*Take in other pleas-in-law for divorce/dissolution of civil partnership as appropriate*]

The pension sharing order sought by the pursuer being justified by the principles set out in s.9(1)(a), (b) and (e) of the Family Law (Scotland) Act 1985 and reasonable having regard to the parties' resources, decree therefor should be pronounced as concluded for.

Pension Sharing Order—Conclusion and supporting averments—Sheriff court F03–11

SHERIFFDOM OF [*sheriffdom*] AT [*place*]

INITIAL WRIT

in the cause

[*name and address*], pursuer

against

[*name and address*], defender

Warrant for intimation to [*name and address of the administrators of the relevant pension scheme: see OCR 33.7(1)(l) or 33A.7(1)(k)*].

The pursuer craves the court to make a pension sharing order providing that the defender's shareable pension rights in the [*scheme*] be subject to pension sharing for the benefit of the pursuer and that the sum of £[*amount*] with interest accrued at the rate of eight per cent a year from [*date of separation*] until the date of transfer of the appropriate pension credit into a qualifying scheme for the pursuer be so transferred.

CONDESCENDENCE

[*Take in Articles of Condescendence of other divorce/dissolution of civil partnership actions*]

The most substantial undivided matrimonial (*OR* partnership) asset is the defender's pension. The defender retired on [*date*]. The defender's date of birth is [*date*]. The pursuer was born on [*date*]. The pursuer was financially dependent on the defender throughout the parties' marriage (*OR* civil partnership). The pursuer made substantial non-financial contributions to the defender and the parties' children during the years when the defender was in employment. The pursuer ran the family home and brought up the children. The pursuer is economically disadvantaged as a result. The pursuer has no personal pension provision. *He/she* will require to provide *himself/herself* with an income for the rest of *his/her* life. The defender's pension is shareable. In the circumstances the order sought for a pension

F03–11 sharing order in terms of which a sum representing 50 per cent of the value of the defender's pension at the date of separation is to be transferred to the pursuer is justified and reasonable.

PLEA-IN-LAW

[*Take in other pleas-in-law for divorce/dissolution of civil partnership as appropriate*]

The pension sharing order sought by the pursuer being justified by the principles set out in s.9(1)(a), (b) and (e) of the Family Law (Scotland) Act 1985 and reasonable having regard to the parties' resources, decree therefor should be pronounced as craved.

Capital sum—Transfer of title—Periodical   **F03–12**
allowance—Interim aliment—Sheriff court—Defences

SHERIFFDOM OF [*sheriffdom*] AT [*place*]

DEFENCES

in the cause

[*name and address*], Pursuer

against

[*name and address*], Defender

The defender craves the court to grant decree ordering the sale of the heritable property at [*address*] and for that purpose to grant warrant to such person as the court shall think proper to dispose of the subjects, heritably and irredeemably, by public roup or private bargain, in such manner and under such conditions as the court shall direct; to ordain the pursuer and the defender to execute and deliver to the purchaser or purchasers of the subjects such dispositions and other deeds as shall be necessary for constituting full right thereto in their persons, failing which to dispense with such execution and delivery and to direct the sheriff clerk to execute such dispositions and other deeds all as adjusted at [*his/her*] sight as shall be necessary aforesaid; and to make such order regarding the price of the subjects when sold, after deduction of any debts or burdens affecting the sale, as to the court seems proper.

ANSWERS TO CONDESCENDENCE

I. [*Respond to the pursuer's averments about jurisdiction, details of the marriage (OR partnership) and grounds of divorce (OR dissolution of partnership) as appropriate.*]

II. Admitted that the matrimonial [*OR* partnership] property includes:
   (i)   the family home at [*address*];
   (ii) the furniture and plenishings in the family home, valued at approximately £[*figure*] at the relevant date;
   (iii) the defender's Army pension with a CETV at the relevant date of £[*figure*], of which are admitted).

£[*figure*] is referable to the period of the marriage (*OR* partnership);

(iv) the parties' joint bank account with the Royal Bank of Scotland, account number [*specify*] which had a balance of £[*figures*] at the relevant date;

(v) the defender's Standard Life policy number [*specify*] with a value of £[*figure*] at the relevant date;

(vi) Volvo registration number [*specify*] registered in the pursuer's name with a relevant date value of about £[*figure*].

Admitted that the parties' liabilities include the following: [*list the parties' liabilities and debts which are admitted*]

(a) standard security in favour of the Royal Bank of Scotland in the sum of £[*figure*];

(b) car loan in the sum of £[*figure*].

Admitted that the pursuer made a non-financial contribution throughout the marriage [*OR* partnership] by staying at home, attending to household duties and caring for the children. Admitted that the pursuer has been dependent upon the defender for financial support during the parties' marriage [*OR* partnership]. Quoad ultra denied. Explained and averred that the pursuer, in addition to the assets mentioned in article II also has the following assets: [*detail*]. The pursuer has worked part time as a [*job*] for an average of [*number*] days per month for the last few years and continues to do so. There is nothing now to prevent the pursuer returning to her old profession. The children are now aged [*age*] and [*age*] years and are largely capable of looking after themselves. The pursuer is only [*age*] years of age and has many useful years of working life ahead. The defender has heavy financial commitments, including an obligation to support his present cohabitee, [*name*], and their child, [*name*], born [*date*]. The defender wishes to have the family home sold and the proceeds divided equally between the parties. The house consists of [*accommodation*] and is too large for the reasonable needs of the pursuer and the children. Were the house to be marketed and the net proceeds divided equally between the parties, the pursuer would be able to buy a flat for herself and the children. The defender is in rented accommodation at a rent of £[*amount in figures*] monthly. He requires his financial share in the family home to enable him to purchase a home for himself, cohabitee and child. In any event, the sums sought by way of capital sum, and periodical allowance are excessive. The defender is agreable to paying a reasonable sum to the

pursuer by way of capital and is prepared to continue F03–12
supporting her financially for a limited period.

III. Admitted that the pursuer qualified as a [*job title*] before
giving up work to bring up the parties' children. Admitted that she is reliant upon voluntary payments of aliment
by the defender of £[*amount in figures*] per month.
Admitted that the defender is a [*job title*] and earns in
excess of £[*amount in figures*] per annum. The pursuer's
outgoings in respect of herself, the children and the family
home are not known and not admitted. Quoad ultra
denied. The pursuer works part time as a [*job*] for an
average of [*number*] days per month. Since the date of
separation, the defender has attempted to provide for both
the pursuer and the children. In addition to the sum of
£[*amount in figures*] per month, which he pays to the
pursuer, he also supports the children at the rate of
£[*amount in figures*] per month each. He pays their school
fees and contributes towards the cost of their school uni-
forms. He takes the children on holiday at least twice a
year. He is willing to continue supporting the children
throughout the years of their education and to provide
reasonable support to the pursuer for a limited period.
The defender supports his present cohabitee, [*name*], and
their child. His outgoings in respect of their accommodation, utility bills, food and household running
expenses are in the region of £[*amount*] monthly. The sum
sought in respect of periodical allowance is excessive.

PLEAS-IN-LAW FOR DEFENDER

1. The order sought for payment of a capital sum not being
justified in terms of s.9(1)(a) and (b) of the Family Law
(Scotland) Act of 1985 and not being reasonable having
regard to the parties' resources, decree therefor should not
be granted as craved.

2. The order for the transfer to the pursuer of the defender's
right, title and interest in the family home and the furniture and plenishings therein not being justified in terms of
s.9(1)(a), (b) and (c) of the said Act of 1985 and being
unreasonable having regard to the parties' resources,
decree therefor should not be granted as craved.

3. The order sought for payment of a periodical allowance

F03–12   not being justified by the principles in s.9(1)(d) and (e) of the said Act of 1985 and being unreasonable having regard to the parties' resources, and an order for payment of a capital sum being sufficient to satisfy the requirements of s.8(2) of the said Act, decree therefor should not be granted as craved.

4. The sum sued for by way of interim aliment being unreasonable decree therefor should not be granted as craved.

5. The order for the sale of the family home being justified by the principle in s.9(1)(a) of the Family Law (Scotland) Act 1985 and being reasonable having regard to the parties' resources, the order sought by the defender should be granted as craved.

Order for sale—Court of Session **F03–13**

IN THE COURT OF SESSION

SUMMONS

in the cause

[*name and address*], Pursuer

against

[*name and address*], Defender

CONCLUSION

For an order for the sale of the heritable property known as and forming [*address*]; for an order ordaining the defender to execute and deliver to any purchaser a valid disposition of [*his/her*] right, title and interest to the property and such other deeds as may be necessary to give a purchaser a valid title to the property and in the event of the defender failing to execute and deliver such disposition and other deeds, for an order authorising the Deputy Principal Clerk of Session to subscribe on behalf of the defender a disposition of the property as adjusted at the sight of the Deputy Principal Clerk of Session, together with such other deeds as may be necessary to give a purchaser a valid title to the property; and for an order for an equal division of the net free proceeds of sale of the property, which failing, for division of the proceeds in such other proportions as the court considers appropriate having regard to the principles of the Family Law (Scotland) Act 1985.

OR

For an order for the sale of the heritable property at [*address*] and for that purpose for a warrant to such person as the court shall think proper to dispose of the subjects, heritably and irredeemably, by public roup or private bargain, in such manner and under such conditions as the court shall direct; for an order ordaining the pursuer and the defender to execute and deliver to the purchaser or purchasers of the subjects such dispositions and other deeds as shall be necessary for constituting full right thereto in their persons, failing which to dispense with such

F03–13 execution and delivery and for an order ordaining the Deputy
Principal Clerk of Session or such other person as the court may
appoint to execute such dispositions and other deeds all as
adjusted at [*his/her*] sight as shall be necessary aforesaid; and to
make such order regarding the price of the subjects when sold,
after deduction of any debts or burdens affecting the sale, as to
the court seems proper.

CONDESCENDENCE

I. (Take in jurisdiction style for divorce or dissolution of civil
partnership. Add articles giving the details of the marriage (*OR* partnership) and grounds of divorce (*OR* dissolution of partnership).)

II. The family home was purchased in [*date*] for £[*amount in
figures*]. It was worth approximately £[*amount in figures*] at
the date of the parties' separation. There is no secured
loan in relation to the property, this having been
redeemed prior to the parties' separation. The defender
continues to reside in the former family home. [*His/her*]
paramour has been residing there with [*him/her*] since
about [*date*]. The pursuer has requested on several occasions, through [*his/her*] agents, that the property be marketed for sale so that the parties' matrimonial (*OR*
partnership) property can be divided. The defender has
consistently refused to entertain such a course of action.
The pursuer requires to purchase suitable accommodation
for [*himself/herself*] for [*his/her*] retirement from [*his/her*]
share of the equity in the former family home. The
defender has considerable resources from both matrimonial (*OR* partnership) and non-matrimonial (*OR* non-
partnership) sources. In all the circumstances the order
sought for sale of the property is justified and reasonable.

PLEA-IN-LAW

The order sought for sale of the heritable property and division
of the net free proceeds of sale equally between the parties,
which failing in such proportions as the court considers
appropriate, being justified having regard to the principle in
section 9(1)(a) of the Family Law (Scotland) Act 1985 and reasonable having regard to the parties' resources, decree therefor
should be granted as concluded for.

Order for sale—Sheriff court

SHERIFFDOM OF [*sheriffdom*]

AT [*place*]

INITIAL WRIT

in the cause

[*name and address*], Pursuer.

Against

[*name and address*], Defender.

The pursuer craves the court:

To grant decree ordering the sale of the heritable property known as and forming [*address*]; to ordain the defender to execute and deliver to any purchaser a valid disposition of [*his/her*] right, title and interest to the property and such other deeds as may be necessary to give a purchaser a valid title to the property and in the event of the defender failing to execute and deliver such disposition and other deeds, to authorise and ordain the sheriff clerk to subscribe on behalf of the defender a disposition of the property as adjusted at the sight of the sheriff clerk, together with such other deeds as may be necessary to give a purchaser a valid title to the property; and to order an equal division of the net free proceeds of sale of the property, which failing, for division of the proceeds in such other proportions as the court considers appropriate having regard to the principles of the Family Law (Scotland) Act 1985.

OR

To grant decree ordering the sale of the heritable property at [*address*] and for that purpose to grant warrant to such person as the court shall think proper to dispose of the subjects, heritably and irredeemably, by public roup or private bargain, in such manner and under such conditions as the court shall direct; to ordain the pursuer and the defender to execute and deliver to the purchaser or purchasers of the subjects such dispositions and other deeds as shall be necessary for constituting full right thereto in their persons, failing which to dispense with such

F03–14 execution and delivery and to direct the sheriff clerk to execute such dispositions and other deeds all as adjusted at [*his/her*] sight as shall be necessary aforesaid; and to make such order regarding the price of the subjects when sold, after deduction of any debts or burdens affecting the sale, as to the court seems proper.

CONDESCENDENCE

I. [*Take in jurisdiction style for divorce or dissolution of civil partnership. Add articles giving the details of the marriage (OR partnership) and grounds of divorce (OR dissolution of partnership).*]

II. The family home was purchased in [*date*] for £[*amount in figures*]. It was worth approximately £[*amount in figures*] at the date of the parties' separation. There is no secured loan in relation to the property, this having been redeemed prior to the parties' separation. The defender continues to reside in the former family home. [His/her] paramour has been residing there with [him/her] since about [*date*]. The pursuer has requested on several occasions, through [*his/her*] agents, that the property be marketed for sale so that the parties' matrimonial [OR partnership] property can be divided. The defender has consistently refused to entertain such a course of action. The pursuer requires to purchase suitable accommodation for [himself/herself] for [his/her] retirement from [his/her] share of the equity in the former family home. The defender has considerable resources from both matrimonial [OR partnership] and non-matrimonial [OR non-partnership] sources. In all the circumstances the order sought for sale of the property is justified and reasonable.

PLEA-IN-LAW

The order sought for sale of the heritable property and division of the net free proceeds of sale equally between the parties, which failing in such proportions as the court considers appropriate, being justified having regard to the principle in s.9 of the Family Law (Scotland) Act 1985 and reasonable having regard to the parties' resources, decree therefor should be granted as craved.

IN THE COURT OF SESSION

SUMMONS

in the cause

[*name, designation and address*], Pursuer

against

[*name, designation and address*], Defender

CONCLUSION

For an order in terms of section 18(1) of the Family Law (Scotland) Act 1985 setting aside the transaction between the defender and [*name*] on [*date*] whereby the defender transferred to [*name*] shares in [*name*] Limited for a sum of £[*amount*].

CONDESCENDENCE

[*Insert appropriate articles.*]

PLEA-IN-LAW

The transaction having had the effect of [or being likely to have the effect of] defeating the pursuer's claim for an order for financial provision [or aliment][1] decree setting aside the said transaction should be granted as concluded for.

---

[1] An application for such an order after final decree shall be made by minute: RCS 49.51.

**F03–16   Setting aside transfer of assets—Heritable property—
Court of Session**

IN THE COURT OF SESSION

SUMMONS

in the cause

[*name and address*], Pursuer

against

[*name and address*], Defender

CONCLUSIONS

[*Insert appropriate conclusions relative to divorce and financial provision including:*]

For an order in terms of section 18(1) of the Family Law (Scotland) Act 1985 setting aside the transaction between the defender and [*name and address*], by means of a disposition dated [*date*] and registered in the Land Register on [*date*] whereby the defender transferred to [*name*] the heritable property hereinafter specified purportedly for a sum of £[*amount*]; for an ancillary order in terms of section 18(4) ordaining [*name*], within 28 days, to execute and deliver to the pursuer a valid (and in the event that such disposition shall attract stamp duty, stamped) disposition of that property, being the subjects at [*address*] together with the garden ground pertaining thereto, and the whole rights, parts, privileges and pertinents effeiring thereto, the title to which is presently registered in the Land Register of Scotland under title number [*number*], giving entry as at the date of decree; and, in the event of [*name*] failing to execute and deliver such disposition, for an order authorising and ordaining the Deputy Principal Clerk of Session to subscribe on his behalf a disposition of the property as adjusted at the sight of the Deputy Principal Clerk of Session.

CONDESCENDENCE

[*Insert appropriate articles including:*]

The parties were joint proprietors of property at [*address*]. By means of a disposition dated [*date*] and registered in the Land Register under title number [*number*] on [*date*] the defender purported to transfer that property to [*name*]. Although that disposition runs in the name of both parties, the pursuer was not aware that such a transaction was being contemplated. She did not sign the disposition. Her signature was not witnessed by [*name of witness*]. The pursuer's signature has been forged. The disposition narrates that the purchase price was £[*amount*]. The pursuer has received no share of any such sum from the defender. The transaction is likely to have the effect of defeating the pursuer's claim for financial provision.

PLEAS-IN-LAW

[*Insert appropriate pleas-in-law including:*]

The defender having entered into a transaction disponing property to [*name*] and that transaction being likely to have the effect of defeating in whole or in part the pursuer's claims for financial provision, decree setting aside the said transaction should be granted as concluded for.

IN RESPECT WHEREOF

F03–17   **Setting aside transfer of assets—Sheriff court**

SHERIFFDOM OF [*sheriffdom*]

AT [*place*]

INITIAL WRIT

in the cause

[*name and address*], Pursuer

against

[*name and address*], Defender

The pursuer craves the court to grant decree in terms of s.18(1) of the Family Law (Scotland) Act 1985 setting aside the transaction between the defender and [*name*] on [*date*] whereby the defender transferred to [*name*] shares in [*name*] Limited for a sum of £[*amount in figures*].

CONDESCENDENCE

[*Insert appropriate articles.*]

PLEA-IN-LAW

The transaction having had the effect of [or being likely to have the effect of] defeating the pursuer's claim for an order for financial provision [or aliment],[1] decree setting aside the said transaction should be granted as craved.

---

[1] An application for such an order after final decree shall be made by minute: OCR 33.52 and 33A.49.

**Unequal division of assets—Special circumstances—Court F03–18
of Session**

IN THE COURT OF SESSION

SUMMONS

in the cause

[*name and address*], Pursuer

against

[*name and address*], Defender

CONDESCENDENCE

I. [*Take in jurisdiction style for divorce or dissolution of civil partnership. Add articles giving the details of the marriage (OR partnership) and grounds of divorce (OR dissolution of partnership).*]

II. The parties' most valuable asset comprises the former family home at [*address*]. This property was purchased in [*date*] for £[*amount*] and title to it is in the parties' joint names. The property is unencumbered by any secured loan. The source of the whole purchase price of the property was provided by the pursuer. She had received a capital settlement on divorce [*OR* dissolution of civil partnership] from her first husband [*OR* civil partner] in [*date*] prior to the parties' marriage [*OR* registration of civil partnership]. The sum did not constitute matrimonial [*OR* partnership] property of the parties. Accordingly the whole source of funding for the parties' family home was the non-matrimonial [*OR* non-partnership] capital of the pursuer. Further, and in any event, the pursuer requires to continue living in the property in order to continue to provide a home for the children of the marriage [*OR* partnership] who are in her care. The nature of the matrimonial [*OR* partnership] asset is accordingly such that it would be unreasonable to expect it to be sold. In the circumstances, it would be fair to share the parties' matrimonial [*OR* partnership] property unequally by awarding the pursuer a greater proportion thereof.

F03–18   PLEA-IN-LAW

The order sought for [*payment of a capital sum/transfer of property/ sale of heritable property*] being justified in terms of s.9(1)(a) of the Family Law (Scotland) Act 1985 and reasonable having regard to the parties' resources, should be granted as concluded for.

Unequal division of assets—Special circumstances— Sheriff court

SHERIFFDOM OF [*sheriffdom*]
AT [*place*]

INITIAL WRIT

in the cause

[*name and address*], Pursuer

against

[*name and address*], Defender

CONDESCENDENCE

I. [*Take in jurisdiction style for divorce or dissolution of civil partnership. Add articles giving the details of the marriage (OR partnership) and grounds of divorce (OR dissolution of partnership).*]

II. The parties' most valuable asset comprises the former family home at [*address*]. This property was purchased in [*date*] for £[*amount*] and title to it is in the parties' joint names. The property is unencumbered by any secured loan. The source of the whole purchase price of the property was provided by the pursuer. She had received a capital settlement on divorce [*OR* dissolution of civil partnership] from her first husband [*OR* civil partner] in [*date*] prior to the parties' marriage [*OR* registration of civil partnership]. The sum did not constitute matrimonial [*OR* partnership] property of the parties. Accordingly the whole source of funding for the parties' family home was the non-matrimonial [*OR* non-partnership] capital of the pursuer. Further, and in any event, the pursuer requires to continue living in the property in order to continue to provide a home for the children of the marriage [*OR* partnership] who are in her care. The nature of the matrimonial [*OR* partnership] asset is accordingly such that it would be unreasonable to expect it to be sold. In the circumstances, it would be fair to share the parties'

F03–19   matrimonial [*OR* partnership] property unequally by awarding the pursuer a greater proportion thereof.

PLEA-IN-LAW

The order sought for [payment of a capital sum/transfer of property/sale of heritable property] being justified in terms of s.9(1)(a) of the Family Law (Scotland) Act 1985 and reasonable having regard to the parties' resources, should be granted as craved.

Varying or setting aside agreement on financial provision—Court of Session

IN THE COURT OF SESSION

SUMMONS

in the cause

[*name and address*], Pursuer

against

[*name and address*], Defender

CONCLUSION

For an order in terms of s.16(1)(b) of the Family Law (Scotland) Act 1985 setting aside the minute of agreement entered into by the parties on [*date*] and registered in the Books of Council and Session on [*date*].

CONDESCENDENCE

I. [*Take in jurisdiction style for divorce or dissolution of civil partnership. Add articles giving the details of the marriage (OR partnership) and grounds of divorce (OR dissolution of partnership).*]

II. Shortly after the parties' separation the defender began to exert pressure upon the pursuer to agree to a sale of the former family home. The defender told the pursuer that it was important that they resolve all financial issues arising out of their separation quickly. The pursuer was receiving treatment for depression. On about [*date*] the defender returned to the family home with a document which [he/she] showed to the pursuer. It was a minute of agreement drafted by the defender's solicitor. The defender persuaded the pursuer that it was in [his/her] interests to enter into the agreement as it contained an obligation on the defender's part to continue to aliment the pursuer at the rate of £[*amount*] until the expiry of a period of five years from the date of separation or until the date of

F03–20   decree of divorce [*OR* dissolution of civil partnership], whichever was later. The pursuer signed the agreement on [*date*] without the benefit of independent legal advice. Clause 2 of the agreement provided that the parties' home would be sold and the proceeds divided equally. Clause 7 provided that the pursuer discharge all claims [*he/she*] might have against the defender for financial provision on divorce [*OR* dissolution of civil partnership]. The minute of agreement is referred to for its whole terms which are held as incorporated herein *brevitatis causa*. The terms of the agreement were unfair and unreasonable at the time they were entered into. No detailed quantification and division of the parties' matrimonial [*OR* partnership] property was considered prior to the subscription of the agreement. The defender had had the benefit of legal advice, unlike the pursuer. The pursuer was suffering from depression and was not aware that the defender's pension entitlement with [*namc*] formed part of the parties' matrimonial [*OR* partnership] property. The defender's pension entitlement as at the date of the parties' separation had a value of approximately £[*amount in figures*]. The pursuer has accordingly been deprived of [his/her] share of a substantial matrimonial [*OR* partnership] asset by entering into the agreement in [*date*]. In these circumstances the order sought to set aside the agreement as not having been fair and reasonable at the time it was entered into is justified and reasonable.

PLEA-IN-LAW

The terms of the minute of agreement not having been fair and reasonable at the time it was entered into, decree setting aside the agreement should be granted as concluded for.

Varying or setting aside agreement on financial provision—Sheriff court   F03–21

SHERIFFDOM OF [*sheriffdom*]

AT [*place*]

INITIAL WRIT

in the cause

[*name and address*], Pursuer

against

[*name and address*], Defender

To grant decree in terms of s.16(1)(b) of the Family Law (Scotland) Act 1985 setting aside the minute of agreement entered into by the parties on [*date*] and registered in the Books of Council and Session on [*date*].

CONDESCENDENCE

I. [*Take in jurisdiction style for divorce or dissolution of civil partnership. Add articles giving the details of the marriage (OR partnership) and grounds of divorce (OR dissolution of partnership).*]

II. Shortly after the parties' separation the defender began to exert pressure upon the pursuer to agree to a sale of the former family home. The defender told the pursuer that it was important that they resolve all financial issues arising out of their separation quickly. The pursuer was receiving treatment for depression. On about [*date*] the defender returned to the family home with a document which [*he/she*] showed to the pursuer. It was a minute of agreement drafted by the defender's solicitor. The defender persuaded the pursuer that it was in [*his/her*] interests to enter into the agreement as it contained an obligation on the defender's part to continue to aliment the pursuer at the rate of £[*amount*] until the expiry of a period of five years from the date of separation or until the date of decree of divorce (*OR* dissolution of civil partnership), whichever

F03–21 was later. The pursuer signed the agreement on [*date*] without the benefit of independent legal advice. Clause 2 of the agreement provided that the parties' home would be sold and the proceeds divided equally. Clause 7 provided that the pursuer discharge all claims [*he/she*] might have against the defender for financial provision on divorce (*OR* dissolution of civil partnership). The minute of agreement is referred to for its whole terms which are held as incorporated herein *brevitatis causa*. The terms of the agreement were unfair and unreasonable at the time they were entered into. No detailed quantification and division of the parties' matrimonial (*OR* partnership) property was considered prior to the subscription of the agreement. The defender had had the benefit of legal advice, unlike the pursuer. The pursuer was suffering from depression and was not aware that the defender's pension entitlement with [*name*] formed part of the parties' matrimonial (*OR* partnership) property. The defender's pension entitlement as at the date of the parties' separation had a value of approximately £[*amount in figures*]. The pursuer has accordingly been deprived of [*his/her*] share of a substantial matrimonial (*OR* partnership) asset by entering into the agreement in [*date*]. In these circumstances the order sought to set aside the agreement as not having been fair and reasonable at the time it was entered into is justified and reasonable.

PLEA-IN-LAW

The terms of the minute of agreement not having been fair and reasonable at the time it was entered into, decree setting aside the agreement should be granted as craved.

Cohabitants—Financial provision on cessation of   F03–22
cohabitation—Court of Session

IN THE COURT OF SESSION

SUMMONS

in the cause

[*name and address*], Pursuer

against

[*name and address*], Defender

CONCLUSIONS

FIRST   For payment by the defender to the pursuer of a capital sum of [*words*] (£[*figures*]) with interest thereon at the rate of eight per cent a year from [*date of separation/date of citation*] or from such other date as the court considers appropriate until payment.

SECOND   For payment by the defender to the pursuer of [*words*] (£[*figures*]) per [*week/month*] in respect of caring for the child of whom the parties are the parents with interest thereon at the rate of eight per cent a year on each [*weekly/monthly*] payment from the date the same falls due until it is paid; and for an interim order at the said rate.

THIRD   For the expenses of the action.

CONDESCENDENCE

I. [*Take in jurisdiction style for divorce or dissolution of civil partnership as appropriate.*]

II. The parties met in [*date*]. They began to live together in [*date*]. They lived together as if they were husband and wife [*OR* civil partners]. They purchased property in joint names. Household bills were paid out of a joint account.

F03–22   The parties' child [*name*] was born on [*date*]. An extract certificate of birth is produced.

III. During the period of cohabitation the parties' property included:

(i)   the house at [*address*] where the parties cohabited, which has a value of £[*figure*];

(ii)   the defender's pension which has a value of £[*figure*];

(iii)   the parties' joint bank account with the Royal Bank of Scotland, account number [*specify*] which had a balance of £[*figure*] at [*date*];

(iv)   the defender's Standard Life policy number [*specify*] a value of £[*figure*] at [*date*];

(v)   Volvo registration number DSF 216 registered in the pursuer's name with a current value of about £[*figure*].

The parties' liabilities comprise:

(a)   standard security in favour of the Royal Bank of Scotland in the sum of £[*figure*];

(b)   car loan in the sum of £[*figure*].

In about [*date*] the defender decided that [*he/she*] wished to attend university with a view to qualifying as a [*specify*]. The pursuer supported the defender's decision. For a period of [*number*] years the pursuer supported the defender financially while [he/she] attended university and was unable to earn an income. The defender has derived economic advantage from contributions made by the pursuer. The pursuer is a qualified [*specify*]. [He/she] formerly worked with [*name*] and earned a salary of [*amount*]. The pursuer's promotion prospects were good. Following the birth of the parties' child [*name*] the pursuer gave up [his/her] employment in order to devote [himself/herself] to looking after the child, the defender and the parties' home on a full-time basis. As a result [his/her] ability to earn a reasonable salary has been diminished. [He/she] has no pension provision. [He/she] has suffered economic disadvantage in the interests of the defender and the parties' child. The defender has been able to advance [his/her] career, having been supported financially by the pursuer to retrain and subsequently having [his/her] home and child looked after free of charge by the pursuer. The defender has been promoted annually. [His/her] salary has been increased annually. [He/she] has a generous pension provision. [He/she] has derived economic advantage from the contributions made in the interests of the family by the pursuer. The economic advantage to the defender in terms of [his/her] gains in **F03–22** income and earning capacity has not been offset by any economic disadvantage suffered by [him/her] in the interests of the pursuer or the child. The economic cost of supporting the pursuer during the child's childhood is less than the market cost of employing a child minder and a house keeper. The defender had an obligation to aliment the child in any event. The economic advantage the pursuer has derived from the defender has been minimal. In financial terms it has been comparable to state benefits, to which the pursuer would have been entitled had [he/she] not cohabited with the defender. The economic disadvantage suffered by the pursuer in terms of wage loss over a period of [*number*] years has been £[*amount*]. The pursuer's pension loss over the same period is £[*amount*]. That disadvantage has not been offset by any economic advantage arising from having been alimented by the defender. In the circumstances the pursuer seeks an order in terms of s.28(2)(a) of the Family Law (Scotland) Act 2006.

IV. The parties' child attends an after-school club which [he/she] greatly enjoys at cost of £[*amount*] per term. The child is a talented tennis player. The child has tennis coaching every Wednesday night and Saturday morning at a cost of £[*amount*] a week. The child attends a tennis coaching course every Easter for two weeks and every summer for four weeks at an annual cost of £[*amount*]. The defender has derived economic advantage from contributions made by the pursuer and the pursuer has suffered economic disadvantage in the interests of the defender and the child. Reference is made to Article III of condescendence. In the circumstances the pursuer seeks an order in terms of s.28(2)(b) of the Family Law (Scotland) Act 2006.

PLEAS-IN-LAW

1. The order sought for payment of a capital sum being justified in terms of s.28(3), (5) and (6) of the Family Law (Scotland) Act 2006, it should be granted as first concluded for.

2. The order second concluded for being justified in terms of s.28(3) of the Family Law (Scotland) Act 2006, it should be granted as concluded for.

F03–22   3. The sum sued for by way of interim order being reasonable decree therefor should be granted as concluded for.

Cohabitants—Financial provision on cessation of   F03–23
cohabitation—Sheriff court

SHERIFFDOM OF [*sheriffdom*]

AT [*place*]

INITIAL WRIT

in the cause

[*name and address*], Pursuer

against

[*name and address*], Defender

The pursuer craves the court:

FIRST   to grant decree for payment by the defender to the
pursuer of a capital sum of [*words*] (£[*figures*])
Sterling with interest thereon at the rate of eight per
cent a year from [*date of separation/date of citation*] or
from such other date as the court considers
appropriate until payment.

SECOND   to grant decree for payment by the defender to the
pursuer of [*words*] (£[*figures*]) Sterling per [*week/
month*] in respect of caring for the child of whom
the parties are the parents with interest thereon at
the rate of eight per cent a year on each [*weekly/
monthly*] payment from the date the same falls due
until it is paid; and for an interim order at the said
rate.

THIRD   to find the defender liable in the expenses of the
action.

CONDESCENDENCE

I. [*Take in jurisdiction style for divorce or dissolution of civil
partnership as appropriate.*]

II. The parties met in [*date*]. They began to live together in

F03–23   [*date*]. They lived together as if they were husband and wife [*OR* civil partners]. They purchased property in joint names. Household bills were paid out of a joint account. The parties' child [*name*] was born on [*date*]. An extract certificate of birth is produced.

III. During the period of cohabitation the parties' property included:
  (i)   the house at [*address*] where the parties cohabited, which has a value of £[*figure*];
  (ii) the defender's pension which has a value of £[*figure*];
  (iii) the parties' joint bank account with the Royal Bank of Scotland, account number [*specify*] which had a balance of £[*figure*] at [*date*];
  (iv) the defender's Standard Life policy number [*specify*] a value of £[*figure*] at [*date*];
  (v)   Volvo registration number DSF 216 registered in the pursuer's name with a current value of about £[*figure*].

The parties' liabilities comprise:
  (a)   standard security in favour of the Royal Bank of Scotland in the sum of £[*figure*];
  (b)   car loan in the sum of £[*figure*].

In about [*date*] the defender decided that [he/she] wished to attend university with a view to qualifying as a [*specify*]. The pursuer supported the defender's decision. For a period of [*number*] years the pursuer supported the defender financially while [he/she] attended university and was unable to earn an income. The defender has derived economic advantage from contributions made by the pursuer. The pursuer is a qualified [*specify*]. [He/she] formerly worked with [*name*] and earned a salary of [*amount*]. The pursuer's promotion prospects were good. Following the birth of the parties' child [*name*] the pursuer gave up [his/her] employment in order to devote [himself/herself] to looking after the child, the defender and the parties' home on a full-time basis. As a result [her/his] ability to earn a reasonable salary has been diminished. [He/she] has no pension provision. [He/she] has suffered economic disadvantage in the interests of the defender and the parties' child. The defender has been able to advance [his/her] career, having been supported financially by the pursuer to retrain and subsequently having [his/her] home and child looked after free of charge by the pursuer. The defender has been promoted annually. [*His/her*] salary has been increased annually. [He/she] has a

generous pension provision. [He/she] has derived eco- **F03–23**
nomic advantage from the contributions made in the
interests of the family by the pursuer. The economic
advantage to the defender in terms of [his/her] gains in
income and earning capacity has not been offset by any
economic disadvantage suffered by [him/her] in the
interests of the pursuer or the child. The economic cost of
supporting the pursuer during the child's childhood is
less than the market cost of employing a child minder and
a house keeper. The defender had an obligation to aliment
the child in any event. The economic advantage the pursuer has derived from the defender has been minimal. In
financial terms it has been comparable to state benefits, to
which the pursuer would have been entitled had [he/she]
not cohabited with the defender. The economic disadvantage suffered by the pursuer in terms of wage loss
over a period of [*number*] years has been £[*amount*]. The
pursuer's pension loss over the same period is £[*amount*].
That disadvantage has not been offset by any economic
advantage arising from having been alimented by the
defender. In the circumstances the pursuer seeks an order
in terms of s.28(2)(a) of the Family Law (Scotland) Act
2006.

IV. The parties' child attends an after-school club which [he/
she] greatly enjoys at cost of £[*amount*] per term. The child
is a talented tennis player. The child has tennis coaching
every Wednesday night and Saturday morning at a cost of
£[*amount*] a week. The child attends a tennis coaching
course every Easter for two weeks and every summer for
four weeks at an annual cost of £[*amount*]. The defender
has derived economic advantage from contributions made
by the pursuer and the pursuer has suffered economic
disadvantage in the interests of the defender and the child.
Reference is made to Article III of condescendence. In the
circumstances the pursuer seeks an order in terms of
s.28(2)(b) of the Family Law (Scotland) Act 2006.

PLEAS-IN-LAW

1. The order sought for payment of a capital sum being
   justified in terms of s.28(3), (5) and (6) of the Family Law
   (Scotland) Act 2006, it should be granted as first craved.

2. The order second craved being justified in terms of s.28(3)

F03–23   of the Family Law (Scotland) Act 2006, it should be granted as craved.

3. The sum sued for by way of interim order being reasonable decree therefor should be granted as craved.

Cohabitants—Financial provision on intestacy—Court of   F03–24
Session

IN THE COURT OF SESSION

SUMMONS

in the cause

[*name and address*], Pursuer

against

[*name and address*], Defender

Warrant to intimate to [*names and addresses*] as persons having
an interest in the deceased's net intestate estate referred to in the
condescendence attached to this summons.[1]

CONCLUSIONS

FIRST   For the transfer of the deceased's whole right, title
            and interest in and to the heritable property known
            as and forming [*address*], together with the furniture
            and plenishings contained therein to the pursuer; to
            ordain the defender to make, execute and deliver to
            the pursuer a valid disposition of the deceased's
            right title and interest to the property and such
            other deeds as may be necessary to give the pursuer
            a valid title to the property and to the furniture and
            plenishings and that within one month of the date
            of decree to follow hereon and in the event of the
            defender failing to make, execute and deliver such
            disposition and other deeds to authorise and ordain
            the Deputy Principal Clerk of Session to subscribe
            on behalf of the defender a disposition of the heri-
            table property as adjusted at the sight of the Deputy
            Principal Clerk of Session together with such other
            deeds as may be necessary to give the pursuer a
            valid title to the heritable property and to the fur-
            niture and plenishings.

SECOND   For payment by the defender to the pursuer of a
            capital sum of [*words*] (£[*figures*]) Sterling with

interest thereon at the rate of eight per cent a year from [*date of citation*] or from such other date as the court considers appropriate until payment.

THIRD For the expenses of the action.

CONDESCENDENCE

I. The pursuer resides at [*address*]. The pursuer formerly cohabited with the late [*name*] (hereinafter referred to as "the deceased") until [his/her] death on [*date*]. The deceased died intestate and domiciled in Scotland. This court accordingly has jurisdiction. The defender resides at [*address*]. The defender is the executor dative[2] of the deceased in terms of a decree granted by [*specify court and location*] on [*date*] and is a person having an interest in the deceased's net intestate estate. [*Names and addresses*] also have an interest in the deceased's net intestate estate. The pursuer seeks warrant to intimate this action to them.

II. The parties met in [*date*]. They began to live together in [*date*]. They lived together as if they were husband and wife (*OR* civil partners). They purchased property in joint names. Household bills were paid out of a joint account.

III. The deceased's net intestate estate comprises:
   (i) a one half pro indiviso share in the heritable property at [*address*];
   (ii) the furniture and plenishings in the heritable property;
   (iii) bank account with the Clydesdale Bank account number [*specify*] with a balance of £[*figure*] at the date of death;
   (iv) investment bond with the Royal Bank of Scotland with a value of £[*figure*] at the date of death;
   (v) 3000 shares in Scottish Power plc with a value of £[*figure*];
   (vi) Jaguar car registration number [*specify*] with a value of £[*figure*].
   The pursuer is the other pro indiviso proprietor. The pursuer and the deceased bought the property in [*date*] as a retirement home for themselves. The disposition to the pursuer and the deceased did not contain a survivorship destination. The deceased was entitled to a pension. The deceased had named the pursuer as the beneficiary on the

pension documentation in the event of the deceased's **F03–24**
death. The pursuer has received £[*amount*] from the pension trustees in consequence of the deceased's death. The
only other claims on the deceased's net intestate estate are
the claims of the defender and the persons named in the
warrant for intimation. They are the children of the
deceased's late cousin. They have had no contact with the
deceased since at least [*date*]. The pursuer and the
deceased were a loving and devoted couple. They were
constant companions for [*number*] years. The deceased
would have wished the pursuer to inherit [his/her] whole
estate. In the circumstances the pursuer seeks transfer of
the property at [*address*] and payment of a capital sum.

PLEAS-IN-LAW

1. The order for the transfer to the pursuer of the deceased's
   right, title and interest in the heritable property and the
   furniture and plenishings therein being justified in terms
   of s.29 of the Family Law (Scotland) Act 2006, decree
   therefor should be granted as first concluded for.

2. The order sought for payment of a capital sum being
   justified in terms of s.29 of the Family Law (Scotland) Act
   2006, it should be granted as second concluded for.

---

[1] RCS 49.8(1)(n).
[2] The deceased's executor must be called as a defender: RCS 49.90.

F03–25 Cohabitants—Financial provision in intestacy—Sheriff court

SHERIFFDOM OF [*sheriffdom*]

AT [*place*]

INITIAL WRIT

in the cause

[*name and address*], Pursuer

against

[*name and address*], Defender

The pursuer craves the court:

1. to grant decree for the transfer of the deceased's whole right, title and interest in and to the heritable property known as and forming [*address*], together with the furniture and plenishings contained therein to the pursuer; to ordain the defender to make, execute and deliver to the pursuer a valid disposition of the deceased's right title and interest to the property and such other deeds as may be necessary to give the pursuer a valid title to the property and to the furniture and plenishings and that within one month of the date of decree to follow hereon and in the event of the defender failing to make, execute and deliver such disposition and other deeds to authorise and ordain the sheriff clerk to subscribe on behalf of the defender a disposition of the heritable property as adjusted at the sight of the sheriff clerk together with such other deeds as may be necessary to give the pursuer a valid title to the heritable property and to the furniture and plenishings;

2. to grant decree for payment by the defender to the pursuer of a capital sum of [*words*] (£[*figures*]) with interest thereon at the rate of eight per cent a year from [*date of citation*] or from such other date as the court considers appropriate until payment;

3. to grant warrant to intimate to [*names and addresses*] as

persons having an interest in the deceased's net intestate **F03–25**
estate[1];

4. to find the defender liable in the expenses of the action.

CONDESCENDENCE

I. The pursuer resides at [*address*]. The pursuer formerly
cohabited with the late [*name*] (hereinafter referred to as
"the deceased") until [his/her] death on [*date*]. The
deceased died intestate and domiciled in Scotland. The
deceased was habitually resident in this sheriffdom at the
date of death. This court accordingly has jurisdiction. The
defender resides at [*address*]. The defender is the executor
dative[2] of the deceased in terms of a decree granted by
[*specify court and location*] on [*date*] and is a person having
an interest in the deceased's net intestate estate. [*Names
and addresses*] also have an interest in the deceased's net
intestate estate. The pursuer seeks warrant to intimate this
action to them.

II. The parties met in [*date*]. They began to live together in
[*date*]. They lived together as if they were husband and
wife [*OR* civil partners]. They purchased property in joint
names. Household bills were paid out of a joint account.

III. The deceased's net intestate estate comprises:
 (i) a one half pro indiviso share in the heritable property
 at [*address*];
 (ii) the furniture and plenishings in the heritable property;
 (iii) bank account with the Clydesdale Bank account
 number [*specify*] with a balance of £[*figure*] at the date
 of death;
 (iv) investment bond with the Royal Bank of Scotland
 with a value of £[*figure*] at the date of death;
 (v) 3000 shares in Scottish Power plc with a value of
 £[*figure*];
 (vi) Jaguar car registration number [*specify*] with a value
 of £[*figure*].
The pursuer is the other pro indiviso proprietor. The
pursuer and the deceased bought the property in [*date*] as
a retirement home for themselves. The disposition to the
pursuer and the deceased did not contain a survivorship
destination. The deceased was entitled to a pension. The

F03–25   deceased had named the pursuer as the beneficiary on the pension documentation in the event of the deceased's death. The pursuer has received £[*amount*] from the pension trustees in consequence of the deceased's death. The only other claims on the deceased's net intestate estate are the claims of the defender and the persons named in the crave for warrant for intimation. They are the children of the deceased's late cousin. They have had no contact with the deceased since at least [*date*]. The pursuer and the deceased were a loving and devoted couple. They were constant companions for [*number*] years. The deceased would have wished the pursuer to inherit [his/her] whole estate. In the circumstances the pursuer seeks transfer of the property at [*address*] and payment of a capital sum.

PLEAS-IN-LAW

1. The order for the transfer to the pursuer of the deceased's right, title and interest in the heritable property and the furniture and plenishings therein being justified in terms of s.29 of the Family Law (Scotland) Act 2006, decree therefor should be granted as first craved.

2. The order sought for payment of a capital sum being justified in terms of s.29 of the Family Law (Scotland) Act 2006, it should be granted as second craved.

---

[1] See OCR chapter 33B.
[2] The deceased's executor must be called as a defender: OCR chapter 33B.

**Varying or setting aside term of agreement on financial   F03–26
provision—Court of Session**

IN THE COURT OF SESSION

MINUTE

in the cause

[*name and address*], Pursuer and Minuter

against

[*name and address*], Defender and Respondent

The Pursuer and Minuter craves the court for an order in terms
of section 16(1)(a) of the Family Law (Scotland) Act 1985 varying
clause [*number*] of the Minute of Agreement subscribed by the
parties on [*date*] and registered in the Books of Council and
Session on [*date*] by reducing the payments of periodical
allowance to be made by the pursuer and minuter to the
defender and respondent in terms of the clause from £[*amount*]
per month to nil, and for the expenses of the application.

STATEMENT OF FACTS

1. The parties were married on [*date*]. They were divorced in
   the Court of Session on [*date*]. This court accordingly has
   jurisdiction.

2. When the parties separated, they entered into a Minute of
   Agreement regulating ownership of the matrimonial and
   other property and making various other provisions of a
   financial nature. Clause [*number*] of the minute of agreement provides for payment by the pursuer and minuter to
   the defender and respondent of £[*amount*] per month by
   way of periodical allowance until her death or remarriage.
   The clause provides for the variation by the court of the
   amount of periodical allowance on the application of
   either party on a material change of circumstances. The
   Minute, subscribed by the parties on [*date*] and registered
   in the Books of Council and Session on [*date*], is referred to
   for its whole terms which are held as repeated herein
   brevitatis causa.

F03–26   3. Since the date of the Minute, and in particular since the date of the divorce, the parties' financial circumstances have changed. The pursuer and minuter was made redundant on [*date*]. In view of his age, it is unlikely that he will be employed in future. He relies on state benefits in the sum of £[*amount*] per week. His weekly expenses are approximately £[*amount*]. He can no longer afford to pay any periodical allowance to the defender and respondent. The defender and respondent is living with a new partner. She works part-time. She is able to support herself financially without payment of periodical allowance. In the circumstances variation of clause [*number*] is justified.

4. The defender and respondent has been called upon to agree that the amount of periodical allowance should be varied to nil, but she refuses or delays to do so. This application is accordingly necessary.

PLEA-IN-LAW

The minute of agreement expressly providing for variation by the court, and variation of the clause being justified in all the circumstances decree should be granted as craved.

IN RESPECT WHEREOF

**Varying or setting aside term of agreement on financial F03–27
provision—Sheriff Court**

SHERIFFDOM OF [*sheriffdom*] AT [*place*]

MINUTE

in the cause

[*name and address*], Pursuer and Minuter

against

[*name and address*], Defender and Respondent

The Pursuer and Minuter craves the court:

1. to grant decree in terms of section 16(1)(a) of the Family
   Law (Scotland) Act 1985 varying clause [*number*] of the
   Minute of Agreement subscribed by the parties on [*date*]
   and registered in the Books of Council and Session on
   [*date*] and that by reducing the payments of periodical
   allowance to be made by the pursuer and minuter to the
   defender and respondent in terms of the clause from
   £[*amount*] per month to nil;

2. to find the defender and respondent liable in the expenses
   of this application.

STATEMENT OF FACTS

1. The parties were married on [*date*]. They were divorced in
   the sheriffdom of [*sheriffdom*] at [*place*] on [*date*]. This court
   accordingly has jurisdiction.

2. When the parties separated, they entered into a minute of
   agreement regulating ownership of the matrimonial and
   other property and making various other provisions of a
   financial nature. Clause [*number*] of the Minute of Agreement provided for the payment by the pursuer and minuter to the defender and respondent of £[*amount*] per
   month by way of periodical allowance until her death or
   remarriage. The clause provided for the variation by the
   court of the amount of periodical allowance on the

F03–27   application of either party on a material change of circumstances. The Minute, subscribed by the parties on [*date*] and registered in the Books of Council and Session on [*date*], is referred to for its whole terms which are held as repeated herein *brevitatis causa*.

3. Since the date of the Minute, and in particular since the date of the divorce, the parties' financial circumstances have changed. The pursuer and minuter was made redundant on [*date*]. In view of his age, it is unlikely that he will be employed in future. He relies on state benefits in the sum of £[*amount*] per week. His weekly expenses are approximately £[*amount*]. He can no longer afford to pay any periodical allowance to the defender and respondent. The defender and respondent is living with a new partner. She works part-time. She is able to support herself financially without payment of periodical allowance. In the circumstances variation of clause [*number*] is justified.

4. The defender and respondent has been called upon to agree that the amount of periodical allowance should be varied to nil, but she refuses or delays to do so. This application is accordingly necessary.

PLEA-IN-LAW

The Minute of Agreement expressly providing for variation by the court, and variation of the clause being justified in all the circumstances decree should be granted as craved.

                              IN RESPECT WHEREOF

**Incidental Elements—Specification of Documents— F03–28
Dissipation of Assets**

SPECIFICATION OF DOCUMENTS

for the Recovery of which a

commission and diligence is sought by

the [*pursuer/defender*]

in the cause

[*name, designation, address*]

PURSUER

against

[*name, designation, address*]

DEFENDER

1. All missives, dispositions, standard securities, deed plans, states for settlement, valuations, calling-up notices and other similar documents relating to the property at [*address*] in the hands of the defender or anyone on his behalf in order that excerpts may be taken therefrom at the sight of the commissioner of all entries showing or tending to show:

   (a) the debt outstanding to the [*name of lender*] at the date of repossession in [*date*];

   (b) the extent of the free proceeds following the sale by the [*name of lender*];

   (c) to whom the free proceeds were paid.

2. All missives, dispositions, standard securities, deed plans, states for settlement, valuations and other similar documents relating to the property at [*address*] in the hands of the defender or anyone on his behalf in order that excerpts may be taken therefrom at the sight of the commissioner of all entries showing or tending to show:

F03–28   (a) the open market value of the property at the date of the sale to the defender's [*e.g. friend/relative*] in [*date*];

(b) the extent of the loan in favour of the [*name of lender*] outstanding at the date of the transfer;

(c) the extent of any agreement between the defender and his [*e.g. friend/relative*] to transfer the property at less than the market value, and whether the difference in values was to be repaid by some other means;

(d) any agreement between the defender and his [*e.g. friend/relative*] to transfer a further [*insert sum*] to him/her;

(e) the extent of the free proceeds of the transfer of the property and to whom they were paid.

3. Failing principals, copies, duplicates or drafts of the above or any of them.

Incidental Elements—Minutes Varying Periodical Allowance F03–29

MINUTE

in the cause

[*name, designation, address*]

PURSUER AND
RESPONDENT

against

[*name, address, designation*]

DEFENDER AND
MINUTER

The Defender and Minuter craves the court:

1. to vary the interlocutor dated [*date*] by varying the rate of periodical allowance payable by the defender to the pursuer from [*sum*] per month to nil; and to vary the interlocutor *ad interim*;

2. to grant the expenses of this minute against the pursuer and respondent in the event of opposition hereto.

STATEMENT OF FACTS

1. By interlocutor dated [*date*] the Lords of Council and Session made an order *inter alia* ordaining payment by the minuter to the respondent of a periodical allowance of [*sum*] per month payable until the respondent's death or remarriage. The minuter now resides at [*address*]. The respondent resides at [*address*]. She has not remarried.

2. Since that date there has been a change of circumstances. The minuter has been in receipt of Jobseekers Allowance since [*date*]. He has no other source of income. He had previously been self-employed as [give details of employment and income, and why these resources are no longer available, and dates of changes]. The minuter has sold assets including his car to meet his living expenses.

F03–29   His bank accounts at [*name of bank*] are overdrawn. His
rent is paid by housing benefit. He has no capital.

3. The minuter has paid periodical allowance at the rate of
[*sum*] a month regularly until recently. He is no longer
able to do so. In the circumstances he seeks variation of
the interlocutor dated [*date*], and variation *ad interim*.

PLEA-IN-LAW

There having been a change of circumstances in terms of section
5(4) of the Divorce (Scotland) Act 1976, the interlocutor should
be varied and varied *ad interim as* craved.

IN RESPECT WHEREOF

Note the terms of RCS 49.49, which refers to rule 49.43. Seven days notice is
required. It is not competent to backdate variations under the 1976 Act: *Sandison's Ex v Sandison*, 1984 S.L.T. 111; *Abrahams v Abrahams*, 1989 S.L.T. (Sh.Ct)
11, *McDonald v McDonald*, 1991 G.W.D. 12– 708; *Wilson v Wilson*, 1992 S.L.T.
664. There is no provision comparable to section 13(4) of the 1985 act, and
section 28(3) does not assist.

**Incidental Elements—Motions—Inspection—Access for   F03–30
Surveyor**

INSPECTION

ACCESS FOR SURVEYOR

On behalf of the pursuer to ordain the defender to allow [*insert name of surveyors*] access to the former matrimonial home at [*address*] in order to survey and value it as at [*date of separation*] and the date of the interlocutor granting the order.

It is permissible to have two dates of valuation: *Demarco v Demarco*, 1990 S.C.L.R. 635. The later value is relevant regarding resources, for section 8(2) of the Family Law (Scotland) Act 1985.

F03–31 Incidental elements—Inhibition on the dependence—Court of Session

IN THE COURT OF SESSION

SUMMONS

in the cause

[*name and address*], Pursuer

against

[*name and address*], Defender

Warrant for arrestment and inhibition on the dependence of the action

CONCLUSIONS

[*Insert appropriate conclusions relating to financial provision or aliment*]

CONDESCENDENCE

I. [*Take in jurisdiction style for divorce or dissolution of civil partnership. Add articles giving the details of the marriage (OR partnership), grounds of divorce (OR dissolution of partnership) and parties' assets and resources.*]

II. The defender not been candid with the pursuer about [his/her] financial situation. In [*date*] the pursuer discovered correspondence from [*name*] showing large deposits into an account in the defender's name. The pursuer asked the defender about this account. The defender thereafter closed the account, transferring substantial amounts to an account unknown to the pursuer. In [*date*] the pursuer received correspondence from the parties' conveyancing solicitor, suggesting that the defender wished access to title deeds over the parties' heritable property. The defender has threatened the pursuer that if [he/she] contacted a lawyer with a view to seeking financial provision [he/she] would not receive any money

at all. The pursuer seeks warrant to arrest and inhibit on **F03–31**
the dependence of this action. In the circumstances there is
a real and substantial risk that enforcement of a decree in
this action in favour of the pursuer would be defeated or
prejudiced by the likelihood of the defender alienating or
dealing with all or some of [his/her] assets were warrant
for diligence on the dependence not granted. Furthermore
it would be reasonable to grant warrant for diligence on
the dependence. The effect on the defender is likely to be
minimal.

PLEAS-IN-LAW

[*Insert appropriate pleas-in-law*]

Add form 14A.2[1]:

Form 14A.2

Statement to accompany application for interim diligence

DEBTORS (SCOTLAND) ACT 1987 s.15D

in the cause

(*name and address*), Pursuer

against

(*name and address*), Defender

STATEMENT

1. The applicant is the pursuer in the action by [*name and address of pursuer*] against [*name and address of defender*].

2. No other persons have an interest.

3. The application [is/is not] seeking the grant under s.15E(1) of the 1987 Act of warrant for diligence in advance of a hearing on the application.

4. The applicant seeks warrant for arrestment and inhibition

F03–31   on the dependence of the action. The grounds on which the applicant makes the application are fully set out in article [*number*] of condescendence which are held as repeated herein *brevitatis causa*.

.... *(Signed)*

Solicitor for [*name and address of pursuer*].

---

[1] Adapt RCS Form 14A.2 as appropriate.

Incidental elements—Diligence on the dependence—Sheriff court

SHERIFFDOM OF [*sheriffdom*]

AT [*place*]

INITIAL WRIT

in the cause

[*name and address*], Pursuer

against

[*name and address*], Defender

The pursuer craves the court:

[*Insert appropriate craves relating to financial provision or aliment*]; and

To grant warrant for arrestment and inhibition on the dependence of the action

CONDESCENDENCE

I. [*Take in jurisdiction style for divorce or dissolution of civil partnership. Add articles giving the details of the marriage (OR partnership), grounds of divorce (OR dissolution of partnership) and parties' assets and resources.*]

II. The defender has not been candid with the pursuer about [his/her] financial situation. In [*date*] the pursuer discovered correspondence from [*name*] showing large deposits into an account in the defender's name. The pursuer asked the defender about this account. The defender thereafter closed the account, transferring substantial amounts to an account unknown to the pursuer. In [*date*] the pursuer received correspondence from the parties' conveyancing solicitor, suggesting that the defender wished access to title deeds over the parties' heritable property. The defender has threatened the pursuer that if [he/she] contacted a lawyer with a view to seeking

F03–32   financial provision [he/she] would not receive any money at all. The pursuer seeks warrant to arrest and inhibit on the dependence of this action. In the circumstances there is a real and substantial risk that enforcement of a decree in this action in favour of the pursuer would be defeated or prejudiced by the likelihood of the defender alienating or dealing with all or some of [his/her] assets were warrant for diligence on the dependence not granted. Furthermore it would be reasonable to grant warrant for diligence on the dependence. The effect on the defender is likely to be minimal.

PLEAS-IN-LAW

[*Insert appropriate pleas-in- law*]

Add form G4A[1]:

Form G4A

Statement to accompany application for interim diligence

DEBTORS (SCOTLAND) ACT 1987 Section 15D

Sheriff Court [*details*]

in the cause

[*name and address*], Pursuer

against

[*name and address*], Defender

STATEMENT

1. The applicant is the pursuer in the action by [*name and address of pursuer*] against [*name and address of defender*].

2. No other persons have an interest.

3. The application [is/is not] seeking the grant under

s.15E(1) of the 1987 Act of warrant for diligence in **F03–32** advance of a hearing on the application.

4. The applicant seeks warrant for arrestment and inhibition on the dependence of the action. The grounds on which the applicant makes the application are fully set out in article [*number*] of condescendence which are held as repeated herein *brevitatis causa*.

.... *(Signed)*

Solicitor for [*name and address of pursuer*].

ADOPTION

Adoption order under section 29 or 30 of the Adoption and Children (Scotland) Act 2007—Petition—Sheriff court F04–01

PETITION

of

[[A.B.] *full name of first petitioner*]

[*insert any previous surname(s)*]

*delete as appropriate

*and

[[C.D.] *full name of second petitioner*]

[*insert any previous surname(s)*]

[*insert address*]

[*or serial number where allocated*]

for authority to adopt the child [*full name of child as shown on birth certificate*]

who was born on [*child's date of birth*]

[*insert child's present address*]

The petitioner(s) crave(s) the court to make an adoption order in his/her/their favour under section 29 [*or* 30] of the Adoption and Children (Scotland) Act 2007, in relation to the child

*and to dispense with the consent of [*name(s) of the natural parent(s)*] on the ground that [*insert grounds*].

The petitioner(s) condescend(s) as follows:

A. The child

  1. The child is [*age of child*] years of age, having been born on the [*specify date*] day of [*specify year*] at [*place of birth*].

F04–01   2. The child is *male/*female.

3. The child is not and never has been married or a civil partner.

4. The child's natural mother is [*full name and address*].

5. The child's natural father is [*full name and address*].

6. The child's natural father has*/does not have* parental responsibilities and rights.

7. *The child has the following guardians:

8. [*name(s) and address(es)*].

9. The child is of [British *or specify*] nationality.

10. The child has not been the subject of an adoption order or of a petition for an adoption order *except that [*insert details of any previous order or application*].

11. *The child is entitled to the following property, namely: [*list property*].

12. The following person/people is/are liable to contribute to the support of the child: [*name(s) and address(es)*].

B. The petitioner(s) and arrangements for the child

1. *The first/second/both petitioner(s) is/are domiciled in a part of the British Islands.

2. *The petitioner(s) reside(s) in a part of the British Islands and has/have been habitually resident there or elsewhere in the British Islands for at least one year prior to the date of this application.

3. The occupation(s) of the petitioner(s) is/are [*specify*]

4. *The petitioners are married or are civil partners and reside [together/apart].

5. *The petitioners are unmarried and are not civil partners but are living together as if husband and wife/civil partners in an enduring family relationship.

6. *The petitioner is a single person living on his/her own. **F04–01**

7. *The petitioner is married to/a civil partner of/living in an enduring family relationship with the natural mother/father of the child.

8. *The petitioner is married/a civil partner/living in an enduring family relationship but seeks to adopt the child on his/her own and the child is not the child of the petitioner's partner.

9. The petitioner(s) is/are [*respectively [*age*] and [*age*] years of age.

10. The petitioner(s) has/have resident with him/her/them the following persons, namely: [*names*]

11. The child was received into the home of the petitioner(s) on [*date*].

12. The child has continuously had his or her home with the petitioner(s) since the date shown in [11] above.

13. *Arrangements for placing the child in the care of the petitioner(s) were made by [*full name and address of agency or authority or person*] and therefore notification in terms of section 18 of the Adoption and Children (Scotland) Act 2007 is not required.

14. *The petitioner(s) notified [*name of local authority notified*] under section 18 of the Adoption and Children (Scotland) Act 2007 of [his/her/their] intention to apply for an adoption order in relation to the child on [*date of notification*].

15. No reward or payment has been given or received by the petitioner(s) for or in consideration of the adoption of the child or the giving of consent to the making of an adoption order.

16. *A permanence order under section 80 of the Adoption and Children (Scotland) Act 2007, with authority for the child to be adopted was made on [*date*] at [*name of the court*].

F04–01 17. *There is no permanence order with authority for adoption in relation to the child.

18. *An order freeing the child for adoption was made on [*date*] at [*name of the court*].

19. *The child has been placed for adoption by an adoption agency within the meaning of section 2(1) (adoption agencies in England and Wales) of the Adoption and Children Act 2002 with the petitioner(s) and the child was placed for adoption [*under section 19(1) (placing the children with parental consent: England and Wales) of that Act with the consent of each parent or guardian and the consent of the mother was given when the child was at least six weeks old] [*under an order made under section 21(1) (placement orders: England and Wales) of that Act and the child was at least six weeks old when that order was made].

20. *Each parent or guardian of the child has consented under section 20(1) (advance consent to adoption: England and Wales) of the Adoption and Children Act 2002 and has not withdrawn that consent.

21. *By notice under section 20(4)(a) (notice that information about application for adoption order not required: England and Wales) of the Adoption and Children Act 2002 (*name of parent or guardian*) [and (*name of parent or guardian*)] stated that he [*or* she *or* they] did not wish to be informed of any application for an adoption order and that statement has not been withdrawn.

C. Undertaking by the petitioner(s)

The petitioner(s) is/are prepared to undertake, if any order is made on this petition, to make for the said child the following provisions, namely: [*specify*]

D. Welfare of the child

The making of an adoption order would satisfy the need to safeguard and promote the welfare of the child throughout the child's life for the following reasons: [*specify*]

*E Productions accompanying the petition

The following documents are lodged along with this application:

(i) extract birth certificate relating to the child.

(ii) *extract marriage certificate relating to the petitioner(s). [*Note: this need be lodged only in the case of a joint application by spouses or where the application is by one spouse.*]

(iii) *extract certificate of civil partnership relating to the petitioner(s). [*Note: this only needs be lodged in the case of a joint application by civil partners or where the application is by one civil partner.*]

(iv) *consent to the adoption by the child's natural mother.

(v) *consent to the adoption by the child's natural father.

(vi) *consent to the adoption by the child's guardian.

(vii) *consent to the adoption by the child.

(viii) *extract of the permanence order with authority for adoption.

(ix) *extract of the order freeing the child for adoption.

(x) *acknowledgement by local authority of letter by petitioner(s) intimating intention to apply for adoption order.

(xi) *report by the adoption agency in terms of section 17(2) of the Adoption and Children (Scotland) Act 2007.

(xii) *report by the local authority in terms of section 19(2) of the Adoption and Children (Scotland) Act 2007.

(xiii) *any other document not referred to above.

[*list documents*]

The petitioner(s) crave(s) the court

1. to grant warrant for intimation of the petition on the natural parent(s) of the child, where their whereabouts are

F04–01   known, and on such other persons, if any, as the court
may think proper;

2. to appoint a curator *ad litem* and, if necessary, a reporting
officer and direct them to report;

3. thereafter, to make an adoption order in favour of the
petitioner(s) under section 28 of the Adoption and Children (Scotland) Act 2007 on such terms and conditions (if
any) as the court may think fit;

4. to direct the Registrar General for Scotland to make an
entry regarding the order in the Adopted Children Register in the form prescribed by him, giving [*name*] as the
forename(s), and the surname of the petitioner(s) or *insert
another proposed surname*] as the surname of [*name*] in the
form;

5. further, upon proof to the satisfaction of the court in the
course of the proceedings to follow hereon, that [*name of
child*] was born on the [*date*] and is identical with the child
named [*full name of child from original birth certificate*] to
whom an entry numbered [*number*] in the Resister of
Births for the Registration District of [*name of district*]
relates, to direct the said Registrar General to cause such
birth entry to be marked with the word "Adopted" and to
include the abovementioned date of birth in the entry
recording the adoption in the manner indicated in the
Schedule to the said Act; and

6. to pronounce such other or further orders or directions
upon such matters, including the expenses of this petition,
as the court may think fit.

....
Signature of first petitioner

....
Signature of second petitioner

....
Signature of solicitor with designation and address

Adoption order under section 29, 30 or 59 of the Adoption and F04–02 Children (Scotland) Act 2007—Response to Petition—Sheriff court

FORM OF RESPONSE

PART A

[*This section to be completed by the petitioner(s) or the petitioner's(s') solicitor or the sheriff clerk before service.*]

Court ref. No. [*specify*]

[*name and business address of solicitor for the petitioner(s) where applicable*]

In an adoption petition/or petition under section 59 of the Adoption and Children (Scotland) Act 2007 brought in the Sheriff Court [*name and address of court*]

[*name(s) or serial number*]
Petitioner(s)

[*name(s)*] **Respondent(s)**

Date of Service: [*date*]

Date of expiry of period of notice: [*date*]

PART B

[*This section to be completed by the respondent or respondent's solicitor, and both parts of the form to be returned to the sheriff clerk at the above sheriff court on or before the date of expiry of the period of notice referred to in Part A above.*]

*delete as appropriate

[*place and date*]

[*designation and address*]

Respondent, intends to

(a) oppose the petition for an adoption order *or under section 59 of the Adoption and Children (Scotland) Act 2007;

(b) *seek an order

F04–02 in the petition against him or her raised by [*designation and address or serial number*], Petitioner(s).

IF YOU INTEND TO OPPOSE THE PETITION, please state here briefly the reasons why the court should not make the adoption order [*or* order under section 59].

[*State reasons*]

Permanence order under section 80 of the Adoption and Children (Scotland) Act 2007—Petition—Sheriff court

PETITION

of

[A.B.] [*designation of local authority*]

[*insert full name of child as shown on birth certificate*] who was born on [*child's date of birth*]

[*insert child's present address*]

[*or* serial number where allocated]

*delete as appropriate

The petitioner craves the court to make a permanence order under section 80 of the Adoption and Children (Scotland) Act 2007, in relation to the child including the mandatory provision

[*and to include the following ancillary provisions [*insert ancillary provisions sought in terms of section 82 of the Adoption and Children (Scotland) Act 2007*]]

[*and to include in that order provision granting authority for the child to be adopted]

[*and to dispense with the consent of [*name(s) of the parent(s) or guardian(s)*] on the ground that [*specify*].

The petitioner condescends as follows:

1. The child is [*age of child*] years of age, having been born on [*date*] at [*place of birth*]

2. The child is [*male/*female].

3. The child is not and never has been married or a civil partner.

4. The child's natural mother is [*full name and address*].

5. The child's natural father is [*full name and address*].

F04–03   6. The child's natural father [has*/does not have*] parental responsibilities and rights.

7. *The child has the following guardians: [*name(s) and address(es)*]

8. *The child has been/is likely to be placed for adoption [*specify*].

9. *The child's case was referred to the Children's Hearing on [*date*].

10. *The child is subject to a supervision requirement under section 70 of the Children (Scotland) Act 1995.

Arrangements for the child

11. *There is no person who has the right to have the child with him or otherwise to regulate the child's residence under section 2(1)(a) of the Children (Scotland) Act 1995.

12. *The following person(s) have the right to have the child living with him/her/them or otherwise to regulate the child's residence: [*name(s) of person(s)*].

but the child's residence with that/those person(s) is likely to be seriously detrimental to the welfare of the child for the following reason(s): [*specify*].

The following documents are lodged with this application:

(i) extract birth certificate in relation to the child;

(ii) *consent of [*name and address*] to the making of an adoption order;

(iii) *consent of the child dated [*date*];

(iv) *local authority report dated [*date*]

Signed ....

[*designation*]

[*date*]

Permanence order under section 80 of the Adoption and   F04–04
Children (Scotland) Act 2007—Response to Petition—Sheriff
court

FORM OF RESPONSE

PART A

[*This section to be completed by the petitioner(s) or the petitioner's(s') solicitor before service.*]

Court ref. No. [*specify*]

[*name and business address of solicitor for the petitioner(s) where applicable*]

In a petition for a permanence order under section 80(1) of the Adoption and Children (Scotland) Act 2007 brought in the Sheriff Court [*name and address of court*]

[*name*] **Petitioner**

[*name(s)*] **Respondent(s)**

Date of Service: [*date*]

Date of expiry of period of notice: [*date*]

PART B

[*This section to be completed by the respondent or respondent's solicitor, and both parts of the form to be returned to the sheriff clerk at the above sheriff court on or before the date of expiry of the period of notice referred to in Part A above.*]

*delete as appropriate

[*place and date*]

[*designation and address*]

Respondent, intends to

(a) *oppose the application for a permanence order *including provision granting authority for the child to be adopted;

(b) *seek an order

F04–04 in the petition raised by [*designation and address*], Petitioner.

> IF YOU INTEND TO OPPOSE THE PETITION, please state here briefly the reasons why the court should not make the permanence order.

> [*State reasons*]

**Permanence order—Minute for variation of ancillary
provisions under section 92(2) of the Adoption and Children
(Scotland)Act 2007—Sheriff court**   F04–05

MINUTE

by

[full name and address]

Sheriff Court [*specify court*]

Court Ref No. [*specify*]

CHILD IN RESPECT OF WHOM PERMANENCE ORDER HAS
BEEN MADE

[full name and date of birth]

The applicant condescends as follows:

*delete as appropriate

1. The applicant is [*name and address of applicant*] who is
   [*details of capacity of person making the application*].

2. On [*date of order*] on the application of [*name of local
   authority*] the sheriff made a permanence order in respect
   of the child in the following terms [*full details of order*].

3. A copy of the permanence order is attached.

4. *The child's case was referred to the Children's Hearing
   on [*date*].

5. *The child is subject to a supervision requirement under
   section 70 of the Children (Scotland) Act 1995.

6. The applicant asks the court to make the following variation to the ancillary provisions of the permanence order
   [*details of variation sought*].

7. The grounds for the application are as follows: [*specify
   reasons for variation*].

F04–05   8. The following supporting evidence is produced [*list reports, statements, affidavits or other evidence produced*].

The applicant asks the court to:

(a) order the applicant to intimate this application to such persons as the sheriff considers appropriate;

(b) appoint a curator *ad litem* and direct him to report;

(c) fix a hearing, if required;

(d) and thereafter to [*details of variation sought*].

Signed ....

[*date*]

[*name, designation and address*]

Permanence order—Minute for amendment of permanence F04–06
order to include provision granting authority for the child to
be adopted under section 93 of the Adoption and Children
(Scotland) Act 2007—Sheriff court

MINUTE

by

[*full name and address*]

Sheriff Court [*specify court*]

Court Ref No. [*specify*]

CHILD IN RESPECT OF WHOM PERMANENCE ORDER HAS
BEEN MADE

[*full name and date of birth*]

The applicant condescends as follows:

*delete as appropriate

1. On [*date of order*] the sheriff made a permanence order in
   respect of the child.

2. The applicant is the local authority on whose application
   the permanence order was made.

3. A copy of the permanence order is attached.

4. *The child's case was referred to the Children's Hearing
   on [*date*].

5. *The child is subject to a supervision requirement under
   section 70 of the Children (Scotland) Act 1995.

6. The applicant asks the court now to amend the permanence order to include provision granting authority for the
   child to be adopted on the following grounds: [*reasons for
   amendment or order*].

7. The following supporting evidence is produced: [*list
   reports, statements, affidavits or other evidence produced*].

F04–06 The applicant asks the court to:

- (a) order the applicant to intimate this application to such persons as the sheriff considers appropriate;

- (b) appoint a curator *ad litem* and reporting officer and direct them to report;

- (c) fix a hearing, if required;

- (d) dispense with the consent of [*name(s) of parent(s) or guardian(s)*] on the ground that: [*specify grounds*];

- (e) and thereafter to amend the permanence order to include provision granting authority for the child to be adopted.

Signed ....

[*date*]

[*name, designation and address*]

Permanence order—Minute for revocation of permanence order under section 98 of the Adoption and Children (Scotland) Act 2007—Sheriff court

MINUTE

by

[*full name and address*]

Sheriff Court [*specify court*]

Court Ref No. [*specify*]

CHILD IN RESPECT OF WHOM PERMANENCE ORDER HAS BEEN MADE

[*full name and date of birth*]

The applicant condescends as follows:

*delete as appropriate

1. On [*date of order*] on the application of [*name of local authority*] the sheriff made a permanence order in respect of the child.

2. The applicant is [*state capacity in which application is made*].

3. A copy of the permanence order is attached.

4. *The child is subject to a supervision requirement under section 70 of the Children (Scotland) Act 1995.

5. The applicant makes the following proposals for the future welfare of the child.

6. [*Set out the circumstances justifying revocation of the order*].

The applicant craves the court to:

(a) order the applicant to intimate this application to such persons as the sheriff considers appropriate

(b) appoint a curator *ad litem* and direct him to report;

F04–07   (c) fix a hearing, if required;

(d) thereafter revoke the permanence order under section 98(1) of the Adoption and Children (Scotland) Act 2007

Signed ....

[*date*]

[*name, designation and address*]

INSTRUCTION FOR USE OF THE COMPANION DISC

Introduction

These notes are provided for guidance only. They should be read and interpreted in the context of your own computer system and operational procedures. It is assumed that you have a basic knowledge of WINDOWS. However, if there is any problem please contact our helpline on 0845 850 9355 who will be happy to help you.

CD Format and Contents

To run this CD you need at least:

IBM compatible PC
CD ROM drive
Microsoft Word 98

The CD contains data files of selected Styles and Suggested Notes from the Appendix of Styles in this book. It does not contain software or commentary.

Installation

The following instructions make the assumption that you will copy the data files to a single directory on your hard disk (e.g. **C:\W.Green\Family Actions and Adoption**).

Open your CD ROM drive, select and double click on setup.exe and follow the instructions. The files will be unzipped to your C drive and you will be able to open them from the new **C:\W.Green\Family Actions and Adoption** folder there.

A shortcut can be created for easy access. To do this navigate to **C:\W.Green.** Right click on **Family Actions and Adoption** and select 'Create Shortcut'. This will create a shortcut folder that can be copied to a more accessible location.

Opening Files

A listing of the files supplied on the disc is given in **_index.htm**.
You will be able to open all files directly from this page.

LICENCE AGREEMENT

Definitions
1. The following terms will have the following meanings:
   "The PUBLISHERS" means W. GREEN & SON LTD, incorporated in Scotland under the Companies Acts (Registered No.SC008894) whose registered office is 21 Alva Street, Edinburgh, EH2 4PS, (which expression shall, where the context admits, include the PUBLISHERS' assignees or successors in business as the case may be) of the other part (on behalf of Thomson Reuters (Legal) Limited incorporated in England & Wales under the Companies Acts (Registered No. 1679046) whose registered office is 100 Avenue Road, London NW3 3PF)
   "The LICENSEE" means the purchaser of the work containing the Licensed Material.
   "Licensed Material" means the data included on the disk;
   "Licence" means a single user licence;
   "Computer" means an IBM-PC compatible computer.

Grant of Licence; Back-up Copies
2.(1) The PUBLISHERS hereby grant to the LICENSEE, a non-exclusive, non-transferable licence to use the Licensed Material in accordance with those terms and conditions.
   (2) The LICENSEE may install the Licensed Material for use on one computer only at any one time.
   (3) The LICENSEE may make one back-up copy of the Licensed Material only, to be kept in the LICENSEE's control and possession.

Proprietary Rights
3.(1) All rights not expressly granted herein are reserved.
   (2) The Licensed Material is not sold to the LICENSEE who shall not acquire any right, sale or interest in the Licensed Material or in the media upon which the Licensed Material is supplied.
   (3) The LICENSEE, shall not erase, remove, deface or cover any trademark, copyright notice, guarantee or other statement on any media containing the Licensed Material.
   (4) The LICENSEE shall only use the Licensed Material in the normal course of its business and shall not use the Licensed Material for the purpose of operating a bureau or similar service or any online service whatsoever.
   (5) Permission is hereby granted to LICENSEES who are

members of the legal profession (which expression does not include individuals or organisations engaged in the supply of services to the legal profession) to reproduce, transmit and store small quantities of text for the purpose of enabling them to provide legal advice to or to draft documents or conduct proceedings on behalf of their clients.

(6) The LICENSEE shall not sublicense the Licensed Material to others and this Licence Agreement may not be transferred, sublicensed, assigned or otherwise disposed of in whole or in part.

(7) The LICENSEE shall inform the PUBLISHERS on becoming aware of any unauthorised use of the Licensed Material.

Warranties

4.(1) The PUBLISHERS warrant that they have obtained all necessary rights to grant this licence.

(2) Whilst reasonable care is taken to ensure the accuracy and completeness of the Licensed Material supplied, the PUBLISHERS make no representations or warranties, express or implied, that the Licensed Material is free from errors or omissions.

(3) The Licensed Material is supplied to the LICENSEE on an "as is" basis and has not been supplied to meet the LICENSEE's individual requirements. It is the sole responsibility of the LICENSEE to satisfy itself prior to entering this Licence Agreement that the Licensed Material will meet the LICENSEE's requirements and be compatible with the LICENSEE's hardware/software configuration. No failure of any part of the Licensed Material to be suitable for the LICENSEE's requirements will give rise to any claim against the PUBLISHERS.

(4) In the event of any material inherent defects in the physical media on which the licensed material may be supplied, other than caused by accident abuse or misuse by the LICENSEE, the PUBLISHERS will replace the defective original media free of charge provided it is returned to the place of purchase within 90 days of the purchase date. The PUBLISHERS' entire liability and the LICENSEE's exclusive remedy shall be the replacement of such defective media.

(5) Whilst all reasonable care has been taken to exclude computer viruses, no warranty is made that the Licensed Material is virus free. The LICENSEE shall be responsible

to ensure that no virus is introduced to any computer or network and shall not hold the PUBLISHERS responsible.

(6) The warranties set out herein are exclusive of and in lieu of all other conditions and warranties, either express or implied, statutory or otherwise.

(7) All other conditions and warranties, either express or implied, statutory or otherwise, which relate in the condition and fitness for any purpose of the Licensed Material are hereby excluded and the PUBLISHERS shall not be liable in contract, delict or in tort for any loss of any kind suffered by reason of any defect in the Licensed Material (whether or not caused by the negligence of the PUBLISHERS).

Limitation of Liability and Indemnity

5.(1) The LICENSEE shall accept sole responsibility for and the PUBLISHERS shall not be liable for the use of the Licensed Material by the LICENSEE, its agents and employees and the LICENSEE shall hold the PUBLISHERS harmless and fully indemnified against any claims, costs, damages, loss and liabilities arising out of any such use.

(2) The PUBLISHERS shall not be liable for any indirect or consequential loss suffered by the LICENSEE (including without limitation loss of profits, goodwill or data) in connection with the Licensed Material howsoever arising.

(3) The PUBLISHERS will have no liability whatsoever for any liability of the LICENSEE to any third party which might arise.

(4) The LICENSEE hereby agrees that
  (a) the LICENSEE is best placed to foresee and evaluate any loss that might be suffered in connection with this Licence Agreement,
  (b) that the cost of supply of the Licensed Material has been calculated on the basis of the limitations and exclusions contained herein; and
  (c) the LICENSEE will effect such insurance as is suitable having regard to the LICENSEE's circumstances.

(5) The aggregate maximum liability of the PUBLISHERS in respect of any direct loss or any other loss (to the extent that such loss is not excluded by this Licence Agreement or otherwise) whether such a claim arises in contract or tort shall not exceed a sum equal to that paid at the price for the title containing the Licensed Material.

Termination

6.(1) In the event of any breach of this Agreement including any violation of any copyright in the Licensed Material, whether held by the PUBLISHERS or others in the Licensed Material, the Licence Agreement shall automatically terminate immediately, without notice and without prejudice to any claim which the PUBLISHERS may have either for moneys due and/or damages and/or otherwise.

(2) Clauses 3 to 5 shall survive the termination for whatsoever reason of this Licence Agreement.

(3) In the event of termination of this Licence Agreement the LICENSEE will remove the Licensed Material.

Miscellaneous

7.(1) Any delay or forbearance by the PUBLISHERS in enforcing any provisions of this License Agreement shall not be construed as a waiver of such provision or an agreement thereafter not to enforce the said provision.

(2) This Licence Agreement shall be governed by the law of Scotland.